The Handbook of Academic Writing

A Fresh Approach

The Handbook of Academic Writing

A Fresh Approach

Rowena Murray and Sarah Moore

Open University Press

Open University Press
McGraw-Hill Education
McGraw-Hill House
Shoppenhangers Road
Maidenhead
Berkshire
England
SL6 2QL

email: enquiries@openup.co.uk
world wide web: www.openup.co.uk

and Two Penn Plaza, New York, NY 10121-2289, USA

First published 2006

Reprinted 2010

Copyright © Rowena Murray and Sarah Moore 2006

A catalogue record of this book is available from the British Library

ISBN-10: 0 335 21933 0 (pb) 0 335 21934 9 (hb)
ISBN-13: 978 0 335 21933 9 (pb) 978 0 335 21934 6 (hb)

Library of Congress Cataloguing-in-Publication Data
CIP data applied for

Typeset by RefineCatch Limited, Bungay, Suffolk
Printed in Great Britain by Ashford Colour Press Ltd., Gosport, Hants.

The McGraw·Hill Companies

For Ger and Morag

Contents

Acknowledgements

We warmly thank all of the following colleagues and friends: Maura Murphy, Sarah MacCurtain, Angelica Risquez, Nyiel Kuol, Helena Lenihan, Margery Stapleton, Eoin Reeves, Eoin Devereux, Liz Devereux, Jill Pearson, Mike Morley, Noreen Heraty, Gary Walsh, Harriet Cotter, Karen Young, Terry Barrett, Gearldine O'Neill and Alison Farrell.

We are grateful to those who took time to discuss, read and comment on our writing-in-progress, including Donald Gillies, Bill Johnston, Caroline Parker, Christine Sinclair and Morag Thow.

Finally, particular thanks to all of the participants of the University of Limerick and University of Strathclyde writers' groups and writers' retreats who, since 2001, have been sharing and developing their academic writing in ways that have created new communities of practice at our universities and beyond.

Preface

If you are an academic, the chances are that your career development is defined by what you write. This simple fact is often the basis of a cynicism and hostility within the academic world. Despite the inevitable problems associated with how writing is evaluated and rewarded across the disciplines, academic writing continues to be seen as the fulcrum on which many other aspects of scholarship depend. In light of this, it is extraordinary that the process of academic writing continues to be an under-explored, unexamined and poorly reflected-upon process. If it is a process that lies at the very centre of academic performance and success for both academic teachers and their students, then surely its dynamics and challenges need to be subjected to more thorough analysis. This book engages in that analysis in order to provide an empowering framework for academic writers. It aims to help you to develop effective approaches to your own writing challenges. It offers insights and lessons that we think will be particularly useful for those who are new to the academic environment, but will also help with the re-conceptualization of writing-related issues for those who have been operating in academic environments for some time.

Academic writing is often a highly problematic but always potentially transformational activity. Despite the great diversity within and between different academic disciplines, several common themes are associated with the experience of writing in academia. It is often encountered as a process that is full of paradoxes. This book aims to identify and explore those common themes and to help you, the academic writer, to address and resolve the paradoxes for yourself. It will do this in a way that can also help you to become a more productive, effective writer with healthier, more positive approaches to what it means to be an academic, and more particularly what it means to be a writer of academic text. Whether you are writing your doctorate, planning a journal article, struggling with reviewers' comments, or drafting a research proposal, this book will help you to make more effective progress. It will help you to devise a strategy that will reach beyond any individual writing task and to develop an integrated approach to your life as an academic, in which writing plays a central role.

Perspective and background of the authors

We are both experienced in the process of academic writing within our own disciplines and have worked with academic writers for many years. During this time, we have identified a range of common fears and problems that people bring to the academic writing process. We have facilitated and witnessed a variety of ways in which academics can experience important breakthroughs in their development as writers. Our motivation in writing this book is to share the approaches that we have found can help to create more productive writing habits among academics. In doing this, we also explore the values and ideas that we believe are necessary to underpin effective academic writing.

The importance of the iterative nature of writing

The idea of writing being driven by an iterative dynamic is central to all of the themes that we explore in this book. We see academic writing as being characterized by a dynamism that is essential but often frustrating for those who are charged with the responsibility of doing it. We demonstrate that effective writers must wane as well as wax, ebb as well as flow, go back as well as go forward. These ideas will be more fully outlined in Chapters 1, 2 and 3, where academic writing is defined in detail, and where the iterative characteristics of writing are explored.

We believe that it is important to understand writing paradoxes in your development as an academic writer. Once you explore and accept the paradoxical nature of writing, and once this is less surprising to encounter, it may be possible for you to confront the challenges of academic writing in some new and interesting ways.

Problems with writing – problems with the academy

The problems associated with academic writing are those that haunt the many creative activities that have become highly 'transaction-based' in organizational settings. The rewards associated with productive academic writing, and the sanctions associated with a lack of it, increasingly form a backdrop to academic life that is often experienced as stressful and threatening (Chandler, Barry and Clark, 2002). Writing can be driven by a negative ethic, and one that is linked to a 'deficiency' model of professional development. 'Unless you have a PhD you can't be a legitimate academic'. 'Unless you publish regularly in a range of identified journals, you won't be promoted.' 'Unless you bring in so much research funding to your department, you won't be a valued member of your academic community.' These are often seen as the realities of academic life. Parts of academia may still offer a privileged existence, but increasingly it comes with a price. And part of that price may be expressed as the pressure to write. Many talk about competition between colleagues that gives rise to dysfunctionally cut-throat dynamics. Many lament that individualistic, non-collaborative behaviour is rewarded and endorsed when they feel that university life should be encouraging just the opposite. Positive writing environments can enhance the possibilities associated with sharing ideas, collaborating, teaching, research and learning. Like several commentators in academic environments, we think that it is time to reframe the nature of academic writing.

For many, academic writing has become a thorn in the side of the academy, instead of the glue that holds everyone together. It can be argued that the emergence of the 'new public management' and the managerialist processes with which corporate values have been implemented has prevented academic writing from being a process through which learning and scholarship are nourished, and through which positive dialogue within and between disciplines is initiated and sustained. We believe that it is still possible for academic writing to represent a route through which teaching, learning and research in universities can be more meaningfully united. We think that reconceiving writing in more positive, collaborative ways offers important solutions to many of the problems that haunt contemporary university settings. From the perspectives of individual academics and from those of organizational developers in universities, we propose that this book offers a set of implementable interventions that could help to give rise to the development and sustenance of healthier approaches to writing.

Influences from other fields of inquiry

In developing our ideas, we refer to a range of both established and emerging ideas from various fields. We explore the fact that, separate from the external rewards with which it may be associated, writing can be satisfying and pleasurable in its own right. We refer to concepts of 'flow' (Csikszentmihalyi, 1990) which define how sheer, unselfconscious delight can be associated with exceptional performance and the activity that is required to achieve it. We refer to the idea that 'transaction-oblivious' orientations like those associated with natural play are those that can direct us towards the achievement of healthy and more meaningful patterns of academic writing. We show through our own experiences and through the accounts of others (for example Grant and Knowles, 2000), that writing can become a pleasurable activity, even for academics who dread the process and initially feel a lack of confidence and competence when it comes to writing within their academic disciplines.

We also believe that many popular ideas such as emotional intelligence (Goleman, 1995), stress management, self-esteem, career development, and the principles of mentoring, networking and coaching can all be incorporated more successfully into both individual and group strategies for developing academic writing. In this book, we will describe a range of interventions through which this can be achieved.

An overview

In Part I, we present a contextualized analysis of academic writing in university and other third-level settings.

Chapter 1 sets the scene by defining and exploring important aspects of academic writing. We explore the iterative nature of writing, which we argue characterizes all writing, and we unravel some of the paradoxes that are an inevitable part of the process. By analysing writing paradoxes, we present a matrix for the development of writing strategies that can form a useful framework for building positive approaches to writing while avoiding unhelpful routines and habits. Chapter 2 focuses on initiating creative, energized and confident approaches to academic writing. The act of 'advancing', or stepping forward, is defined as a phase in which ideas are plentiful and when a large range of possibilities and alternatives lies in front of the writer. This orientation requires preparation and planning, and you will be introduced to techniques to generate and free up your thought processes. You will be encouraged to explore the positive dimensions of the 'creative phase' as well as to understand that this phase can also be associated with problems such as those associated with disorganization, chaos and information overload. Chapter 2 ends with a series of practical ideas about how writers can get ready to step forward in their academic writing processes.

In Chapter 3 we discuss why retreating, or stepping back and regrouping after sustained advances in writing, is an essential part of the process. In that chapter, we also provide an analysis of what retreating from your writing requires. Retreating may be initiated by your own independent discoveries or as a result of critical insights from someone else. Chapter 3 also presents a structured strategy for developing healthy attitudes and responses to criticism. You will be encouraged to explore how to make the most of stepping back from your writing by understanding the positive and negative experiences associated with this phase, and by developing effective methods of re-evaluating your writing. Chapter 4 explores the importance of understanding your own particular academic discipline when you are targeting the places in which you hope to have your work published. It identifies common and distinctive features of scholarship and proposes specific ways in which these features can be incorporated into your academic writing.

Part II provides details of three innovative approaches to developing academic writing in third-level settings. Chapter 5 describes the conceptual and practical considerations associated with running university-based 'writers' retreats'; Chapter 6 provides details of a structured 'writing for publication programme'; while Chapter 7 explores the parameters associated with the establishment of writers' groups to enhance and develop effective academic writing. Chapter 8 explores the insights gained from these institutional innovations in order to redefine and reconceptualize writing practices in academia, with particular reference to the importance of community-based, collaborative learning both for faculty and students.

Part III focuses on how you can renegotiate your academic life in very practical ways, ensuring that writing occupies a central part of your professional life, linking positively with a whole range of other important activities. We show that by becoming a more productive writer, you can enhance your roles as a teacher and a scholar. We suggest that in order to proceed with your academic writing, it is useful to engage in a series of negotiations that recognize not just your responsibilities, but also your rights within your own unique network of professional and private support. The final chapter of this book pulls together the strands and themes that have been explored to present practical models of academic writing that can act as guides to help you to put academic writing in context and manage its peaks and troughs effectively.

Some of the ideas we present in this book are simple and self-evident. Some will provide you with strategies that you have never thought of before, but which we hope you can easily and rapidly adopt to help to develop your writing. More simply, though, all of them encourage you to enjoy the journey. They urge you to stop always looking at your watch and to avoid the constant temptation to measure the distance between your current position and your ultimate destination. The more you focus on the journey and its intricacies and sights, the faster and more exciting the journey will feel.

If you struggle with academic writing, or associate it with at least some bad experiences, we hope that this book will help you to reframe the aspects of the academic writing process that you find difficult. If you have already gained a good command of your academic writing, we hope that some of the reflections in this book will help to generate even more comfortable writing routines and to enhance your approach further. If you are interested in helping others to develop their academic writing, then this book will also provide some insights for you to consider. Throughout this book, we encourage academic writers, educational developers and teachers of academic writing, to consider ideas, rhythms and routines that they may not have previously considered in this way or this deliberately. Importantly, if you approach writing as a linear, step-by-step process and you can't bear the thought of 'going back' to revisit and to re-evaluate your writing, then we hope that this book will offer some workable alternatives that will feed and develop your approach as a writer. We hope that the reflections, strategies, guidance and advice that this book contains will help to make your academic writing effective, pleasurable and satisfying – characteristics that should be central to the experience of academic life.

Part I

In getting to grips with the process of academic writing, a useful starting point is to explore its nature, phases and characteristics. If we know more about the complexities of the process, it may be that we can come to terms with the challenges of the content. These first four chapters have been written in order to engage in a deeper analysis of writing paradoxes, writing time slots, writing progression and writing regression. Getting used to the idea that writing has its inherent complexities and rhythms is, we think, a useful thing to do. So this first part of the book recognizes that while every single writing task will have its own unique cadences and rhythms, there are characteristics of academic writing that are common to many people's experience, the central elements of which we have tried to capture in this part of the book.

1

Defining and understanding academic writing

Introduction • The iterative, continuous nature of academic writing •
Exploring the paradoxes of academic writing • Tackling writing time frames
• Writing exercises • Guidance for defining your own writing challenges

Introduction

This chapter provides a framework for exploring the dynamics and paradoxes of academic writing. It presents guidelines that can help you to analyse your academic writing processes, but also emphasizes that no amount of theorizing and intellectualizing of writing is going to make more successful writing patterns unless accompanied by an undertaking to engage in practical strategies and to plan effective writing tactics. Equally, though, in order to generate practical approaches to writing, we have found that academic writers can benefit from exploring some of the contradictions and paradoxes associated with the academic writing process. Academics who have taken the time to participate on our writing programmes have often reported that examining what writing means to them, and analysing its paradoxes and contradictions, helps them to gain more control over how, when and what they write. You may find it useful too. Also once you have examined more closely the things that bring you to a writing task and the things that take you away from it, you may simply be in a better position to write productively and well.

Exploring writing complexities and paradoxes might help you to make more sense of your experiences of writing and gain more control over its associated processes. Writing has often been described as a demanding and sometimes troublesome dimension of academic life. Analysing its complexities and paradoxes may help to shed more light on why this is the case for many academics in many different contexts.

In order to explore and highlight the complexities and paradoxes that are associated with writing, we first explore its iterative, continuous nature, emphasizing how important we think it is to treat academic writing in a recursive way. We explore writing paradoxes in an effort to explicate the ups and downs of the academic writing process, and we provide a more practical framework within which to manage those paradoxes by introducing the idea of outlining and designing short bursts of effective writing into busy academic life as well as availing of opportunities for longer periods of writing, if such opportunities arise.

The iterative, continuous nature of academic writing

However difficult and complicated it may be, the process of becoming a writer is an important journey. It is a journey that leads us to many new discoveries about ourselves, about our ideas, about the world in which we live, and about our professional identities as academics, teachers, researchers and scholars.

Choosing not to write in academia should not be seen as a principled stand to resist the increasing demands of the academy (though we can understand why people would make that choice for those reasons). Rather, choosing not to write can be conceptualized as an implicit acceptance of an academic half-life in which one's legitimate scholarly voice has not been sufficiently exercised, or respected. To put it more positively, choosing *to* write in one's area of academic expertise is an affirmative choice that announces both your courage and active engagement in the world you have chosen to occupy.

There are many ways in which you can avoid pitfalls and false starts in your writing. There are practical and positive ways in which it can integrate with the other activities in your life. Academic writing can be conceptualized less as 'jumping through hoops' and more as the proactive positioning of your academic voice. By actively addressing questions about your writing – 'How is writing learned?' 'How do people organize themselves in order to write?' 'What are the common difficulties that people encounter, and why?' 'And how can you develop a workable orientation towards academic writing that allows you to fit it into the context of your busy professional and personal life?' – you can help to position it as a controllable and achievable part of your professional development.

Essential to addressing such questions is the recognition that writing is not a single, homogenous, linear achievement towards which you strive and at which you one day arrive. Rather, it is the manifestation of your professional learning journey and it is (or at least it should be) a continuous process involving reflection, improvement, development, progress and fulfilment of various types and in varying measures. It contains different processes and phases, and it is an activity that can help to grease the wheels of your professional life of all sorts of ways. It is not something that needs to interfere with other goals or be psychologically daunting even (or perhaps especially) when you're not doing it.

Focusing on the necessary stages and phases of your writing and what happens to you at different parts of the process may provide you with important learning milestones from which you can benefit just as much as you can from a final, polished written product. If you consider that writing is an iterative process with phases of progression and phases of regression, you might allow yourself to conceptualize your own writing challenges more fruitfully. Reflecting on what many researchers and theorists suggest is the iterative nature of writing may also help you to devise realistic, appropriate and ultimately productive writing strategies. If you have already developed strategies that work for you, then reflecting on the process of writing may help you to enhance and refine them even more.

Your writing can be a companion to your learning rather than an imposing enemy that constantly needs either to be agonizingly wrestled or artfully avoided. There are pleasurable, positive possibilities embedded in every writing task, no matter how onerous such tasks may sometimes feel.

Many commentators have hinted at the paradoxes associated with academic writing. Giving these paradoxes some explicit attention may help you to know what to expect about the contradictions and complexities that writing sometimes contains.

The ebbs and flows, and highs and lows of writing are things that you may already be familiar with, or they may be discoveries that are lurking just around the corner. Whether you are an experienced writer or someone grappling with academic writing for the first time, we believe that it is important for you to be able to recognize many of the conundrums the experience of writing may contain.

Academic writing is not the printed display of one's fully formed thoughts. It starts with flawed, incomplete, vague hunches, ideas and concepts. But, if you exploit its inherent 'revisability', it allows you to come full circle, to revisit ideas long after you first thought of them, to explore the same things in different ways, to experiment, to revise, to repeat and to reconceptualize – all of these are arguably central to the essence of scholarship which you exercise every day in other academic tasks like teaching, supervision and guiding students.

Even if your goal is to produce a perfect piece of writing (an imposing target that may prohibit initial attempts at writing, but one that many writers pursue nonetheless), then surely it is the imperfections, discoveries and serendipitous loops in which you must engage to reach that goal that are at least as interesting as your final destination?

As a starting point, we often encourage academic writers to try to enjoy their writing journeys a bit more than they often say they normally do. Many colleagues find this idea immediately appealing – a sort of antidote to the notion that writing is part of the drudgery of academic work. When invited to consider the enjoyable, positive, creative, empowering aspects of academic writing, many of them respond by saying that even simply associating these words with their writing makes them feel more positively orientated than they might otherwise have been.

But not everyone responds in this way, and perhaps you don't either. In any session that focuses on this orientation, some people tell us that our encouragement is unrealistic. They say it sounds evangelical and not reflective of the realities in which they work. They say that academic writing is neither a positive nor an empowering experience for them, and no amount of trying to convince them that it can be will change that.

These are reactions that we have reflected upon and explored in our work as writing developers. Suggesting that writing, even that which is extremely scholarly, does not actually have to be a fearsome grind and that for many writers can become just the opposite, is something that seems to confront a relatively common view among academics, many of whom see writing as an unpleasant but necessary activity. This idea exists across many different college and university settings. Our response is this: if writing is something that you have to do, but something that you dislike, perhaps it is worth exploring alternative perspectives. Perhaps it is worth analysing your negative associations in order to understand them better. And even if you don't particularly dislike the writing process, you may still have encountered problems and pitfalls that a more thorough analysis of writing and of its processes and paradoxes might help to address.

Exploring the paradoxes of academic writing

Writing involves starting, progressing and finishing a complicated, challenging combination of tasks. It requires you to activate lots of different skills and orientations, sometimes at different stages and phases in the process, sometimes all at the same time. Some researchers have claimed that writing can be experienced as one of the most difficult of all skills, requiring an intricate combination of neurological, physical, cognitive and affective competencies (see, for example, Levine, 2004). Others (perhaps most notably Elbow and Belanoff, 2000) claim that even if writing makes complicated demands on your skills and abilities, it is possible to make writing easy, or at least easy enough for it to feel worth tackling regularly and with good effect.

We share Peter Elbow's optimism that all academics can write and that they can all write well. But this does not take away from the need to recognize the different and contradictory pushes and pulls associated with the writing process.

Writing involves starting and finishing, both requiring very different kinds of orientation. Writing requires listening to and being guided by the voices of others, but also it demands your confidence and your willingness to present your own voice, your own perspectives and your own interpretations. Writing often involves an intimate familiarity with the minute details of a specific piece of work, but it also demands that we position these minutiae on a broader stage, identifying and explaining connections and comparisons in a wider theoretical context. Writing is not just influenced by what we know and what we have discovered about a particular phenomenon, it is also influenced by what we feel, and more particularly, what we feel about ourselves (Boice, 1988). The creative part of writing requires chaos, serendipity and coincidence; but in order to shape and craft our writing effectively, it needs the imposition of at least some order and discipline. The implications of these paradoxes are important and worth exploring in some more detail.

The paradoxes of academic writing

Paradox 1: The **starting** versus **finishing** paradox
Paradox 2: The **originality** versus **convention** paradox
Paradox 3: The **logic** versus **emotion** paradox
Paradox 4: The **easy** versus **difficult** paradox
Paradox 5: The **public** versus **private** paradox

Paradox 1: The starting versus finishing paradox

The starting versus finishing paradox exists by virtue of the fact that the skills associated with starting a writing project are qualitatively and radically different from the skills you need to activate in order to progress and to complete it. Starting a writing project is very different from persisting and finishing, and this fact is often the cause of writing obstacles as the demands of moving from starting to finishing become difficult to overcome.

Many lecturers, professors and academics sit guiltily on a store of unfinished business. They have writing projects that they started once, perhaps long ago, projects that may have had magnificent initial momentum, but for a variety of reasons, the excitement and energy of the early ideas fizzled out and came to nothing. Of course some unfinished doctorates, research papers, journal articles and book chapters out there were terminated for the right reasons, but very many merited a completion that never materialized.

Many of us start our writing projects with at least some enthusiasm and self-belief, but the good intentions and animated beginnings don't always translate into a finished product, and as a result, a lot of the work that went into the early stages of a project does not bear fruit, at least not in any explicit or satisfactory way.

Why do many of us have projects that we start but don't finish? Academic writing often leads people into a zone that can be psychologically dangerous – a zone that human nature impels us to avoid. These dangers are not necessarily apparent initially, but can become very obvious once a writing project is under way. Unless we rise above our initial fears and reactions by building in our own 'safety mechanisms' to guide our writing projects, things can happen that lead us to abandon some of our most promising work.

And indeed it is easy to become overwhelmed by criticism at a crucial stage in the process. This can be precipitated by things like bad reviews or by suddenly being challenged to answer a critical or fundamental question that you hadn't previously considered. As you become more familiar with the field in which you are writing, it is possible to develop a disillusionment about the added value of your work that causes you to cast aside a project altogether when a simple re-orientation could have turned it around. A lack of clarity about the conventions of the genre can set you back, and often it is difficult not to separate your writing from other dimensions of your academic or professional life, making it feel disjointed from the rest of your work.

At certain points in the writing process, you might be too hard on yourself by aiming higher than is appropriate for your stage of development or prematurely exposing your work to highly critical readers. Conversely, in order to protect yourself from excessive criticism, you can become timid and unwilling to expose your work to scrutiny that might help to improve it. Other reasons for stagnant, unfinished work relate to the common and inevitable distractions of life that take you away from your writing projects for longer than you had expected, only to discover on returning that you have lost whatever spark it was that originally encouraged you to get going.

In addition, some academics regularly say that they have become very disenchanted with the requirements and conventions of academic writing, feeling that it is somehow strangling their 'true' voices in so far as it seems to require a stilted and constrained way of expressing ideas, and that conforming to the conventional requirements of 'genre' somehow undermines integrity.

Writing for academia may be conceived as a game that some simply choose not to play. If, however, you feel that academic writing is important to you, either for pragmatic or idealistic reasons (or both), it is vital to realize that these obstructions can be navigated, negotiated and overcome. A starting point may simply be to make writing safe, or at least safe enough for you to keep doing it.

Perhaps initially, the most important dynamics for you to conquer are those that get you started, whatever those initial, sometimes chaotic, sometimes stumbling efforts require. But it is also worth remembering at those initial stages that the maintenance and final closure of your writing tasks require a different set of dynamics that will involve rewriting, editing, revisiting and reconceptualizing. Starting is one thing, but finishing is entirely another. You need to orientate your approaches to writing in ways that will help you to do both successfully.

Paradox 2: The originality versus convention paradox

The originality versus convention paradox reflects the differences and tensions between taking in information and putting forward or articulating ideas of your own. When writing you need to find your own individual voice in the midst of other voices, many of which seem more expert and more knowledgeable than your own. Of course other academic voices do need to be invoked when you write and they do inform and nourish your writing, but they should not drown, smother or sideline the essence of your own contributions. It is perhaps the quest to 'fill a gap' in the literature that makes academic writing sometimes feel so daunting, especially in a context where conventional ways of expressing ideas sometimes appear to be rigid and unyielding. How can fresh ideas and new insights be incorporated into a writing style that tends to demand so much conformity?

You do need to recognize the genres and conventions of your discipline in academic writing (see Murray, 2004). However, you need also to guard against being 'terrorised by the literature' (Becker, 1986) in ways that rob you of your own ideas or that make you less confident about the things that you are trying to say in your own words. The paradox of originality and convention suggests that all academics risk becoming engaged in an endless, defensive trawl of the 'literature' in order to demonstrate what you're saying is completely new or that it fills the elusive 'gap' that is often the intimidating holy grail of academic pursuit. This dynamic can create an insurmountable writing block that stands imposingly between you and your efforts to write.

On one side of this paradox is the reality that if you are too detached from the literature or half-hearted in your efforts to familiarize yourself with it, then you run the risk of 'reinventing the wheel' and, more importantly, of exposing yourself to the unnecessary criticism of more informed counterparts. On the other is the fact that if you are too concerned about the conventions of your discipline and the voices of those who have contributed most convincingly to it, then you run the risk of aligning your work so closely to prevailing giants or popular names in your field that there is really no room left for the fresh voice or the interesting angle that you might otherwise have adopted.

Of course you need to pay attention to the existing literature in the field you have decided to tackle, but you also need to recognize that you are capable of bringing something new and important to that conversation. Be informed by the literature, not constrained by it. Be guided by the prevailing or established voices but not enslaved by them. Listen carefully to the voices of others and read what they have written, but clear your throat, stretch your fingers, and prepare to talk and write yourself. No matter how much you conform to the conventions of your discipline, it is still possible for you to make your contribution with your own unique and original voice.

Finding a confident voice in the great ocean of existing voices is perhaps one of the fundamental rites of passage that academics need to navigate. This rite of passage is never more obvious than when you sit down to write.

Paradox 3: The logic versus emotion paradox

The logic versus emotion paradox is contained in the reality that academic writers are required to cast a cold and objective eye on the nature and contribution of their writing, and yet it is impossible (and also undesirable) to ignore the important emotional dimension that can drive, motivate and influence written work in both positive and negative ways.

In our experience as writing developers, we have found that the logic versus emotion paradox is usually more intense and more impacted than academic writers are initially prepared to admit. But there is plenty of evidence to suggest that it may cause more difficulties for academics than might first appear to be the case.

During the professional writing development workshops that we have facilitated with many academics from all over the world, conversations about the writing process sooner or later touch on the emotional dimensions of writing for academic audiences. People talk about experiencing emotions as extreme as guilt, fear, anxiety, worry, anger and shame when they delay their writing or when they feel for whatever reason that their academic writing is 'not good enough'. Similarly they talk about joy, satisfaction, curiosity, happiness, even euphoria associated with the successful engagement in and completion of their challenging writing tasks. Just as Becker (1986), Boice (1997), Cameron (1999), Grant and Knowles (2000) and others have found, we can only conclude what we knew intuitively already: writing is an issue of the heart as well as the head.

A published research paper does not display the scars that its writer incurred while producing it (not being stained with blood, sweat or tears – at least, not usually). The final product does not reveal the real frustrations, nor does it expose the considerable anxieties or joys to which at least some of its existence can be attributed. When you read academic text written by someone else, you can be deceived by its clarity, its structure and its coherence. You might assume that it was produced easily and fluently. This assumption is likely to be wrong.

The best writing emerges from the writer's willingness to address their own weaknesses, to take on board criticism and to redraft their work several times before completing it.

In order to apply both logical and emotional intelligence to your writing, it's worth engaging in an effort to incorporate emotional awareness into the writing process. The logical dimensions of enhancing or developing a written piece may be significantly blocked because of our emotional reactions and associations. Goleman (1995) reminds us that to any relevant stimulus in our lives we have an emotional reaction before we apply intellectual logic or cognition to it. This can explain some of the reasons why suggestions for revision by peer reviewers of written work can be misinterpreted or ignored. Keep in mind that as well as the logic associated with your academic writing (which includes addressing questions such as: what is the evidence supporting my argument?; what are the bases of my conclusions?; what are the assumptions upon which my assertions are based?; what is my intellectual contribution?; and so on), there are other important questions that reflect the emotional relationship you have developed with your writing. These might include: what are my feelings about this piece of writing in particular, or about the academic writing process in general?; why am I feeling like this at the moment?; how can I harness my emotions in a way that will help me to make progress on this?; is some of what I am feeling preventing me from tackling certain aspects of this task? am I under particular pressure to produce scholarly work? how is this affecting the way I feel about my writing tasks? We're not suggesting that you tangle yourself up in psychotherapeutic babble about writing or become self-indulgent about the processes that it requires. We are, however, asserting that if you ignore the emotional aspects of the act of writing, you miss out on an important opportunity to become a more self-aware and reflective academic writer.

Paradox 4: The easy versus difficult paradox

Writing can seem both easy and difficult at different stages in the process, or even at the same time.

Peter Elbow suggests a variety of reasons why academic writing can feel hard and easy at different points in the journey or even at the same time. It is hard because of all of the things that you are likely to think about when engaged in writing. In academia this is particularly true. The range of audiences that might read what you have written, the types of questions that might be asked or things that might be said about your writing and about you, and the kinds of rewards that you might or might not obtain, depending on how your writing is received, are all considerations that might, at the very least, make you feel uneasy as you attempt to craft your writing. Such considerations paralyse many people's efforts to become productive academic writers. But if you strip away these things and just think about the simple act of writing itself, you might be able to see the other side of this paradox more clearly. Writing can be easy, and even though there may be difficult aspects associated with it, there are features of writing that make dimensions of it intrinsically easy, or at least easier than other forms of expression. Firstly, no one ever has to see what you have written if you don't want them to. And secondly, you are much more in control of what you want to say because you can draft and redraft something in a way that is impossible during a conversation, a meeting or a lecture.

Perhaps a key strategy, then, is for you to become more knowledgeable about when you need to make the writing process easy for yourself, and when you need to encounter its more difficult aspects. If you become more explicitly aware and reflective of what phase of the writing process you are involved in, you will be better able to control and inject 'easy' writing into the writing moments in which you need a kick-start, and to address 'difficult' writing when you need to craft, clarify, inform or adjust the text you have produced.

It is possible that you can navigate the 'easy versus difficult' paradox by recognizing that doing something with ease doesn't mean that it is necessarily simple or unchallenging. Ease implies enjoyment, poise and confidence. These are the kinds of states associated with gaining proficiency in any task that is important to us. In order to develop command over a task, we need to start in ways that are easy, or at least easy enough.

Paradox 5: The public versus private paradox

In a desirable society, the private and the public rituals must both enhance and restrain one another. (Norman, 1995: 85)

Boyer (1990) refers to scholarship as something that demands public scrutiny, something that is by its very essence defined by an inherent openness to criticism, debate and dialogue. Indeed, it can be argued that if you are not prepared to subject your written work to the scrutiny of others, then you're simply in the wrong game. And to some degree, most academics seem to have encountered this rather uncompromising orientation towards their writing.

Our work in helping people to develop their writing confirms that, against this Darwinian backdrop, there should be private, protected writing places that allow academic writers to become more accustomed to the heat to which their work may ultimately be exposed. To put it another way: academic writing doesn't all have to be fire and brimstone associated with the fear of invoking the potential fury of unknown, unnamed experts who you imagine are laughing mirthlessly at your best efforts. If you set up spaces, times and environments for your writing that are private, safe and supportive, then you can equip yourself with the armour and confidence you need when exposing your work to more exacting critics. If you co-opt friendly critics from the very start, then you can provide a built-in antidote to the dangers and anxieties of public scrutiny. Public scrutiny only feels dangerous if you are not equipped to respond to it. If you are, then it can become an exhilarating part of the process of scholarship.

By recognizing that you have at least some control over the privacy that can protect your early writing efforts, you can contain your fragile early drafts, while also building your own self-belief that allows you to consider 'going public' at some specified point in the future (Cameron, 1999). One way of doing this is to identify times when private writing can feed the process more productively than writing for a public audience would. Freewriting, a technique popularized by writing experts such as Flower and Hayes (1977), Elbow and Belanoff (2000), and Murray (2004), is a strategy that can get your writing juices flowing, and involves short private writing sessions (5 to 10 minutes in duration) in which you respond in writing to your own prompts as continuously as possible in order simply to get your ideas down on paper. This type of writing ignores structures, genres, and conventions in order to give rise to a more fluent approach to any writing task. Once you get used to setting up private spaces for your writing, in which you may be freer to play around with ideas and to have a dialogue with yourself about your perspectives on a subject, you can then make advances by picking which nuggets in your private writing world can travel into a more public domain. As one writer puts it:

> The first time I write a draft of a paper . . . I totally let go and rant and rave and say unprofessional things, including swear words. Later I go back and change it to something more acceptable for my academic audience. My theory is that the new, more professional words will still carry the original energy of the first draft, and so even my final 'academised' version will have more oomph than if I tried too hard to control my initial reactions the first time round.
>
> (Cassity via Elbow and Belanoff, 2000: 387)

Remember also that the benefits of keeping your writing to yourself have been underestimated in academic settings. While it is often useful to show your work to people who can help you to improve it, we also know that there are times when such exposure can feel dangerous and problematic, and can lead to blocks that might not have occurred if you had kept it private even for a little longer. It is important sometimes to let yourself write in a private space where any kind of scrutiny is not a consideration or a cause of concern. As Ralph Norman (1995) puts it:

> [Sometimes] we want to be able to hide the precious information under the jacket, or to read it in whispers to the beloved, or to bury it for a while in the vegetable garden. Part of what free people mean by the freedom of appearance is having the power to turn away betimes from where all the others are.
>
> (Norman, 1995: 85)

This is an important insight for helping you to reflect on your writing. If you are so aware of the public performance or output at which your writing is targeted, you may find that your voice lacks personal integrity and becomes nervous and self-conscious. But if you are only immersed in the private, solitary process of writing, it may make the process of 'stepping forward' almost impossible. You could find that simply being aware of a need to balance the public and private dimensions of your academic writing enables you to manage your writing with more confidence and self-determination.

All of these writing paradoxes tend to be under-explored and unspoken in academic contexts, and yet they may help you to find important keys to developing a more self-aware approach to your own academic writing tasks. Just being motivated to write is not enough. We believe that it is important to understand the dynamics of academic writing, and the difficulties that such dynamics can present in the context of your career. In order to develop more comfortable, regular and successful approaches to your academic writing, we encourage you to grapple with these dynamics and paradoxes and to identify which ones are most relevant to your experiences or plans.

Tackling writing time frames

When we have asked colleagues what they need in order to write, they identify a range of things that would help, including mentor support, training, inter-action with experts in their field, conference attendance and funding. But by far the most common response they provide to the question of what would help them to write is 'more time'. Like all areas of human endeavour, writing is inextricably time bound. But it is possible to use and even to manipulate time in ways that support your writing more effectively.

You may find it useful to identify different kinds of writing time zones in which you can productively engage, and to carve up scheduled time for writing in ways that will help you turn good starts into productive finishes.

You can be productive and unproductive in short bursts or long swathes of writing

The literature on effective academic writing has not reached a consensus on whether long swathes of writing are better or worse than short bursts. Some writers say that they can only write when they have 'cleared' a fairly significant block of time in their lives in order to pursue their writing. Others say that allocating long periods of time exclusively to writing (apart from being impractical) risks giving rise to a relentless, intensive approach to writing that leads to burnout, exhaustion and in some cases a sense of isolation that is difficult to climb out of once it is over. Boice (1990), Murray (2004) and others have often highlighted the benefits of 'snack' writing, arguing that long swathes of writing have been shown to be less productive and more psychologically destabilizing than short bursts. However, there are models from the creative writing world that suggest that time away from normal schedules and rhythms of life may be necessary to make progress on certain kinds of writing tasks (see Chapter 5 for an operational example). Zerubavel (1999) encourages academics to find a balance between excessively short and excessively long writing sessions. He suggests that:

> When trying to establish the optimal length of your writing sessions, be sure to take into account two major ergonomic factors; the approximate amount of time it usually takes you to get into a creative mode and the approximate amount of time you can effectively sustain such a mode and be productive. Considering the first factor, of course, ought to help you avoid scheduling writing sessions that are too short. Considering the second should likewise help preclude ones that are too long.
>
> (Zerubavel, 1999: 18)

Writing in short bursts or long swathes often depends on the rest of your schedule at different times in the year. Whether or not you can put aside days, weeks or months exclusively for writing is something that depends on the realities and responsibilities associated with the rest of your life. For practical, work-based reasons, most academics find it very difficult to identify blocks of time in which they can write to the exclusion of everything else. They usually have to deal with a huge range of different activities on a day-to-day basis. The multiple roles played by academics mean that, increasingly, finding time for writing becomes a difficult task in itself (Chandler, Barry and Clark, 2002).

We argue that instead of insisting that short writing snacks are necessarily 'better' than long writing tracts, we can move from one mode to another in effective ways if and when the possibilities for doing so present themselves.

Short writing bursts can be potentially unproductive, but if organized and planned well can form an essential part of an integrated writing strategy. Similarly, longer dedicated periods of writing time can be ultimately unproductive if undertaken without necessary supports and strategies, but planned intensive periods of writing can nourish, develop, accelerate, complete or otherwise sustain essential writing tasks.

Short, unproductive bursts of writing occur when:

- You make insignificant changes to something that has already been written, perhaps borne of a reluctance to let it go, or a lack of confidence about what you're attempting to say. (See, for example, Hjortshoj's (2001) description of the 'endless introduction'.)

Table 1.1 A matrix for developing your writing strategy

	Negative	**Positive**
Small amounts of writing	False starts Disjointed bits of writing Not feeding into the bigger plans that you have for your writing Continuous tinkering with a final draft	Short periods of regular writing Feeding regularly into a larger project Filling in the gaps of an outline
Large blocks of writing	Writing endlessly and without breaks Producing large tracts of text without reflecting or feeling confident about what has been written Writing under pressure	Scheduling and preparing for larger tracts of writing time Feeding writing snacks into a more dedicated period of writing Having crucial periods of time where total focus on writing is achieved

- You do little bits of potentially excellent writing that you don't integrate or capture in a way that is organized enough for you to exploit or develop.
- You identify the kernel of a great idea and write it down somewhere, but never revisit it.

Essentially this kind of writing occurs when you make trivial changes without making progress, or identify important potential writing activity without pursuing or integrating it. We have found that many academics engage in writing that can be described in this way.

Long, unproductive bursts of writing occur when:

- You engage in a lot of endless, feverish writing that takes up time and energy, but may not be well paced, structured or reflected upon.
- You write without breaks, through mealtimes and to the exclusion of other aspects of your life.
- You produce large tracts of text on your own and without at least some advice or observation from others (making you vulnerable to a subsequent writing block).
- You 'write yourself into a corner' and don't know how to get out of it.

The energy and intellectual focus that writing requires can mean that people become too intense in their efforts to write, less likely to share the writing content or process with others and less likely to see reasonable options for changing, redirecting or developing our writing in ways that could make it better. We have encountered many examples of this kind of writing among academics and believe that such an approach can be transformed into more effective and ultimately productive orientations.

Enhanced writing orientations

Short bursts of productive writing

This is an organized, planned approach to writing. It facilitates fitting short, healthy blasts of writing into your daily academic life without feeling that you have to cordon off large tracts of time in order to make progress. It's not productive to do short bursts in random, disorganized ways. In order to become a successful 'short burst writer', you need to spend preparatory time outlining and organizing your work, creating headings, sub-headings and sections, and then working in a deliberate way to fill in the gaps during small specified periods of time. These sessions can be as brief as 20 minutes and may be no longer than an hour each day. If you practise and learn to engage in planned writing bursts, you'll find that your ideas and energy will be less likely to go to waste, that you're more likely to feed your academic writing strategy in a way that pays off for you, generates more coherence in your life, and is simply more effective and efficient.

Long swathes of productive writing

Occasional large tracts of writing time can complement the short burst approach in an integrated way. There may be times in a particular writing project when it will be very helpful to cordon off a larger block of time in order to achieve focus and to make significant progress. Chapter 5 outlines a formal institutional intervention that can facilitate extended, focused writing time in a collaborative setting, but even without the availability of such an intervention, individual academics can benefit from scheduling time out for the progression, acceleration or completion of a writing task. It is often during these scheduled times that crucial breakthroughs can be achieved and opportunities for developing or extending the work can be identified.

Writing exercises

1 To explore the iterative nature of writing, write a summary of your writing project four different times according to these instructions:
   a. A brief, broad outline that might include words, bullet points, ideas. Complete an outline sketch of your writing project that might simply be a series of headings, words or concepts.

b. A 250-word summary that begins with the following words: 'this piece of writing does not. . .' and that focuses on what your writing will not do or will not achieve.

c. A 250-word summary that begins with the following words: 'this piece of writing aims to achieve the following objectives', and continues, 'it does this in the following ways . . .'

d. A flowery exposition: a very wordy, elaborate and ornate piece that is about four times as long as the ones you wrote for summaries b and c. Expand the number of words you need to explain or discuss your ideas. Indulge yourself by making your writing as wordy and lengthy as possible. Don't worry if your sentences are too long – this exercise is about elaborating and extending your ideas. Then trawl through this wordy piece to see if there are any new nuggets or ideas from which your writing could benefit.

Reflect briefly on the writing exercises you have just completed: which of the four did you find the most difficult? Which was the easiest? Where did you get 'stuck', and where did you find yourself writing most fluently and with most comfort? When we ask writers to do these exercises, they often report that it helps them to diagnose their difficulties and to highlight the areas in which they are most confident. If you find it difficult to say what your writing is not about, then you may still need to set clearer boundaries around your work. If you find it difficult to specify how your writing achieves its objectives, then you may need to do more work in sequencing and linking your work. If you particularly liked writing exercise d, then you may benefit from exploring more alternatives and possibilities associated with your work.

2 Recognizing the emotional and logical dimensions of your writing: again, think about a writing project in which you are currently involved or on which you are considering embarking:

a. On one sheet of paper, write down all the things you feel about this writing project: the positive and the negative.

b. On another sheet of paper, imagine yourself as your own supportive reviewer or supervisor, and write down all the things you think logically about this writing project (for example, do you still need to gather more data?; do you have a good idea about what other literature guides your thinking on this?; are you knowledgeable about research and opinion in other areas?). What are the main conclusions you think you are likely to be able to articulate at this stage in the writing project? Logically speaking, what needs to be done in order to progress and finish this work?

c. Now revisit the 'emotional' page and see if your 'logical brainstorm' invokes or changes any of your negative emotions by implying positive action or next steps. Write a brief plan and schedule that will help you to take those steps.

3. Invoking your own writing paradoxes: perhaps the discussion in this chapter on writing paradoxes has prompted you to identify other paradoxes
inherent in the writing process. We have selected only a few for detailed
discussion, but of course there are many others that overlap and extend the
paradoxes that we have identified: generate a list of other paradoxes that
might be relevant as you tackle writing projects. They might include some
of the following:
   a. cloning versus creativity (Murray, 2004);
   b. discipline and flexibility; ideals and constraints (Zerubavel, 1999);
   c. product and process (Hjortshoj, 2001);
   d. order and chaos (Csikszentmihalyi, 1990);
   e. safety and danger (Cameron, 1999).

Guidance for defining your own writing challenges

- We have often observed that different writers find certain paradoxes more
  evocative than others. Reflect briefly on which paradoxes are most meaningful for you and think about how this insight might help you to start
  developing or enhancing your own academic writing strategy.
- Once you have identified writing paradoxes that are most relevant to your
  own writing experiences, you may be in a better position to design your
  own approach to writing in a way that suits your needs more appropriately.
- If a sense of safety or danger in writing is most evocative for you, then
  perhaps these are the features that you need to address most crucially in
  your writing by creating safer spaces, recruiting a supportive mentor and
  doing more private, contained writing. Perhaps also you need to examine
  critically how helpful your current writing mentors are.
- If striking a balance between discipline and flexibility is more of a struggle,
  then issues like time management and the ordering and structuring of your
  work may need more attention.
- Analyse the writing paradoxes identified in this chapter to help develop
  more effective writing strategies for yourself, recognizing that you may need
  to adopt a different approach than the ones you see other people using.

2

Advancing your writing

Starting, gaining momentum and engaging creatively in the academic writing process

Introduction • Initial reflections on the advance phase • Exploring the motivation to write • What do academics like about writing? • What do academics dislike about writing? • The elements of enjoyment • Creativity • When you just don't know where to start – experimenting with different kinds of writing • The downside of advancing • How to get started and become creatively engaged with your academic writing – checklist and strategy

Introduction

The purpose of this chapter is to consider how academic writers get started, gain momentum and engage creatively in the writing process. We have chosen to call this the 'advance' phase. It involves stepping forward with your writing task, and we have seen that this is an identifiable, creative and crucial phase of writing. It is characterized by writing that is initially unbridled by any explicit concern about structure, coherence and rhetoric. It is associated with and emerges from the first steps taken towards the beginning of a writing task. It involves the generation and maintenance of the initial spark that feeds your writing. It is characterized by novelty and interest: new ideas, new directions, new beginnings and new insights. Any aspect of your writing that is marked by a feeling of moving forward, of generating newness and of creative engagement is relevant to this aspect of the writing dynamic.

Initial reflections on the advance phase

Understanding this aspect of writing involves asking these kinds of questions: how do you (or how will you) start writing?; how do you gain confidence in your writing and maintain levels of interest and motivation that keep you writing regularly?

Advancing might begin as a conversation about something that you might like to write about, or it might be as concrete as producing text according to an outline you have defined in some detail. Taking something from your head, or from an idea or from a snatched conversation or an insight from a lecture or an angle that you have identified from your own research or from the work of others, does contain an element of risk. Advancing, then, needs to be imbued with enough excitement and motivation to make it a risk that you feel is worth taking.

It is important when reflecting on your writing to understand the first early stages of your writing tasks. These first steps will often determine the momentum and direction that you may subsequently gain in pursuit of any writing goal. As you start a writing project, sometimes you might feel confused and uncertain, sometimes you will feel confident, comfortable and ready, sometimes you will feel trepidation, sometimes excitement. The advance phase may last only for 10 or 15 minutes, or you might stay in that zone for days, or even longer. Always, though, it will be a process of going forward, even when you later, temporarily but inevitably, need to retreat again. The more engaged and the less fearful you feel at these early stages, the more likely it will be that your progress will be positive and progressive. Before you subject your work to criticism and to more rigorous requirements of academia, it may be necessary simply to get something down on paper. Advancing means doing just that.

The psychology of beginning or of injecting more creative engagement into your academic writing requires you to orientate yourself in a range of ways. In getting ready to write, there need to be periods of productivity in which you must write *before* you're ready, or at least before you *feel* ready, in order to overcome obstacles to your fluency, your generation of ideas, and your confidence as a writer (Boice and Jones, 1984; Murray, 2004). In starting to write, and in becoming engaged and 'present' in your writing, we think it is useful to explore some important psychological processes such as motivation, creativity and the conditions for engaged action. These are all concepts that we suggest are central to the necessary phase of advance in pursuit of the production of academic writing.

Exploring the motivation to write

We suggest that academics might find it useful to reflect on their motivation in an effort to gain more control over why they do (or why they don't) write. By analysing your motivation to write, you may be able to start creating better conditions for academic writing. If you think about the times when you are really committed to and engaged in any activity, then you might be able to start theorizing about what generic factors need to be in place in order for you to feel engaged, switched on, focused and motivated when you write.

> **Reflecting on your writing: what do you like and dislike about academic writing?**
>
> Before reading the next section, briefly write down anything you can think of that you like about academic writing – include anything you feel and think about the writing process and consider any recent experiences you have had with writing. Once you have done this, write another list. This time focus on the things you dislike about the writing process. Use these lists of likes and dislikes to reflect on how you might further develop your own writing strategy and to compare your insights with those outlined below.

Some behavioural theorists have suggested that in order to be motivated to start anything, you need to perceive that there are at least some associated rewards that respond to your particular needs (see, for example, Morley et al., 2004). If you find that it is hard to get started, or that something always seems to intervene between you and a writing task, it may be that you don't perceive that the rewards are valuable enough. If, for example, you have already gained academic tenure, if you have reached a level of promotion with which you are happy, or if promotion and/or tenure are simply not that important to you, then the career rewards that are sometimes associated with academic writing may not be the kinds of rewards that will give you the spark you need to begin and sustain your writing tasks.

However, even when you do perceive that there is real value in the rewards that might be linked to academic writing, you may be demotivated for other reasons. The rewards associated with academic writing might be things that you see are 'out there', but you may be less confident that these rewards will ever apply to you, even if you do start writing. This is a motivational contingency that behavioural theorists call 'effort-reward probability' (see, for example, Porter and Lawler, 1968). A lot of academic writers we have worked with seem to perceive that their own effort-reward probability is very low. This can be true even for academics who have been relatively successful in producing and publishing written output, but it is particularly true for new academic writers. As one novice writer put it: 'it just seems like such a lottery: you engage in all this effort and all this angst, and finally produce something. Then you send it off, and it's rejected, and you're back to square one. Eventually, it's easier to stop doing that to yourself and to concentrate on other things like teaching and supervising well.'

In order for you to be motivated to write, and to keep writing, it is important that you perceive that your effort-reward probability is somewhere above nil. It is worth reflecting on the fact that increasing your likelihood of becoming a regular, productive academic writer won't happen unless you write. Writing well, or at least in ways that will be accepted and endorsed by those people who review your work, is another matter, one that you can address in due course (see Chapter 4). But in order to write well, you must first write (Cameron, 1999). Perhaps this simple truism might start to challenge any sneaking notion that effort-reward probability is too low for you to bother. If after every step you take in the direction of a particular destination, you say 'I'm not there', then you risk de-energizing and discouraging yourself. It's true that initial writing efforts don't bring you immediately to your destination, but we can almost guarantee that they do get you closer. If you want to be self-critical, don't tell yourself you're not there. Instead, tell yourself you're not there *yet* and then keep going.

Starting to write is a necessary step, but it's not sufficient to produce effective outputs (such as finished pieces and published papers). In order for your efforts to turn into effective performance, you need to have a clear idea about what other work is associated with academic writing (e.g. research, analysis, discussion within your field of inquiry). If you operate in an academic setting, it is likely that you will get guidance on the nature and quality of research in your area. But in our experience, it is less likely that you'll be guided specifically on things such as what academic writing in your field should look like and how you can improve your chances of getting published. You will be able to enhance your skills and abilities in these areas in particular by reading Chapters 3 and 4 of this handbook. In the meantime, it is worth keeping in mind that enhancing your motivation to write requires more than just improving your technical writing skills.

Even when you have produced and published a piece of academic writing, there may be no guarantee that you'll be motivated to do it again. Unless there are actual (as opposed to expected) rewards that emerge as a result of a written piece, you may feel that there's not much point in continuing. It is rare (though not unheard-of) that a single piece of academic writing represents a lever that activates rewards such as promotion, tenure and invitations to speak at international conferences. Usually such extrinsic rewards emerge as a result of a range of published pieces which, taken in combination, may give rise to accolades and recognition bestowed by decision-makers who have the power to endorse your work. But no matter how effective your writing and publishing strategy currently is, or no matter how effective it eventually becomes, there are no guarantees that these rewards will automatically accrue to you. The political dynamics, the changing competitive criteria, and the unequal (and unfair) distribution of rewards are realities in all organizations, not least (or maybe especially) in academic ones. Don't always rely on the notion that the more effective and productive you are as an academic writer, the more likely it is that someone will reward you for it. In any case, these rewards may not be as effective as other things that could drive and energize your writing strategies.

Research on motivation (Kohn, 1993) has demonstrated that most extrinsic reward systems are basically flawed and ultimately incapable of motivating performance. Rather, it seems to be the case that the excessive reliance on extrinsic rewards can make people feel controlled and manipulated in ways that sooner or later they tend to reject. Intrinsic rewards (that is, those that come from within yourself) relate to experiences such as curiosity, satisfaction, knowledge development and an increased sense of efficacy (White, 1959). These may be much more powerful and effective drivers of your own writing behaviour. For the academic writers whom we have studied, we have certainly found that the more enjoyable aspects of writing tend to relate more to intrinsic rewards, but that they also consider that extrinsic rewards are at least somewhat relevant and meaningful.

The following two sections represent a summary of over a hundred responses that we have gathered from academic writers. You will probably find that some of these insights relate to your own experience of writing, but perhaps your own list of likes and dislikes will have added a few more.

What do academics like about writing?

Our findings suggest that there are four 'writing drivers' that are commonly invoked reasons why academics like to write (or at the very least, why they like some aspects of the writing process). These drivers are associated with the following factors: interactivity and dialogue; knowledge creation and extension; achievement, output and approval; and the intrinsically pleasurable experience of 'flow'.

We will explore each of these writing drivers in some more detail in order to examine the role that each can play in sustaining and nourishing your efforts to advance your own academic writing.

Interactivity and dialogue

Academic writing affords you the opportunity to interact and discuss ideas with a wider audience. As you develop knowledge and understanding of your field, the excitement of being able to share your ideas, build on those of others, ask experts what they think and engage those within the discipline with your topics and perspectives becomes more relevant. At the beginning, you may feel that you have very little to say, but after making initial advances in your writing you have at least created a situation in which dialogue with others is both more possible and more likely. When academics start to get their work published, they put themselves in a situation where engaged and interested others are more likely to encounter their work. The dialogue of your discipline moves outside of the classroom, in which relatively small numbers of your students are exposed to your ideas (or your interpretations of the ideas of others), and into a wider realm where your ideas and contributions may simply receive more airplay.

Of course, this is not always what people experience as a direct result of their academic writing, but when they do, it seems that the effect on their continued motivation to write is both positive and strong. As one academic put it:

> the buzz that I get from someone writing to me with a question about my writing, or even better, ringing me up from another country to discuss something that I have written, is so fabulous. What starts to happen is that you begin to realise that you become part of an endless conversation to which you have made some small contribution, which in turn catalyses contributions from others and . . . helps you learn more and understand more. For me, this kind of dialogue is the essence of continuous learning.

It seems that it is not just the interactivity that is sometimes possible with academic writing, but also the *iterativity* that we have argued from the beginning of this book represents an important and potentially motivating aspect of academic writing and which echoes in many of the other pleasurable writing drivers that academics have identified.

However, it is also true to say that many academics feel more than a little cynical about the capacity for their writing to give rise to high-quality dialogue (or indeed any dialogue whatsoever). They wonder what the point is of writing for academic journals that few people will read and fewer still will derive any benefit from. For as long as academia has existed, the benefits of academic writing have been questioned. As Van den Berghe (1970) once put it: 'The average academic author does not write because he has something to say, because he hopes to contribute to knowledge, or because he has fun doing it; rather he writes and publishes in order to improve his c.v'. (p. 87). If this is your starting point too, if your primary concern is to build a more impressive CV, you should not feel guilty about that. The system is set up in such a way as to make this a very common motivator of writing. What our own findings suggest, however, is that when asked to identify what they like about writing, the need to build their CV and the associated pressure to write are rarely invoked. On the other hand, the pleasure of engaging in scholarly dialogue, and the extent to which writing affords more chances to do that are regularly cited as reasons why writing is motivating.

As you step forward to tackle a writing task, you may well be keeping pragmatic, career-building considerations in mind, but it is the opportunity for engaging in the dialogue that is more likely to keep you at your desk, to nourish and sustain your motivation, and to help you derive pleasure out of the tasks and activities that writing entails.

Knowledge creation and extension

The process of writing is not just an outcome of thinking, it also helps to feed the thinking process, and to give rise to new insights and angles on the material you are tackling. One of the reasons that people often feel blocked when writing for academia is the inherent assumption that they have to think very carefully about what it is that they are going to write, and to perfect these thoughts before ever putting pen to paper. As Hjortshoj (2001) puts it, academic writers feel nervous because they feel that: 'critical readers are waiting for you to make a false move'. The very process of writing both extends and creates knowledge (Flower and Hayes, 1977; Mullin, 1989). And furthermore, it's one of the reasons that academic writing can be pleasurable, not punishing (Bean, 2001). If you see writing as something that is part of your professional learning, rather than simply a measure of your professional performance, then your motivation and your catalysts for writing might be stronger.

Achievement, output and approval

The sense of achievement and delight associated with finishing written work makes people feel proud and effective. There's nothing wrong with the satisfaction associated with adding another published piece of work to your CV. Academics say that they enjoy this sense of completion and achievement. There is a satisfaction and pride associated with seeing your name in print – it might just encourage you to keep going and to try again or to step up your academic writing strategy. Being congratulated about having achieved an academic writing goal is something that really does feel good. Organizational theorists have long recognized that one of the drivers of human behaviour is the experienced need for achievement (see, for example, McClelland, 1961; and Fisher and Yuan, 1998). This can be both intrinsically motivating (in that the achievement is accompanied by an internal sense of satisfaction and completion) and extrinsically reinforcing (in that it may give rise to recognition, congratulation and reward). However, in the light of this motivator, it is worth reminding you again that if you come to expect that a successful written piece will automatically lead to praise, promotion or pats on the back of other kinds, then you may be installing a cycle of disappointment into your writing experiences that may ultimately make you very disillusioned about your contribution, your outputs and the nature of academia in general. If you're going to make writing a regular, satisfying, professionally developing and sustaining activity, then you're going to need more than the fragile promise of external reward to spur you on. And yet endorsement for your written outputs does undoubtedly add to the strength of the sense of achievement that goes with that output. Therein lies another of the paradoxes of academic life. We think that the key to addressing this paradox is first to be aware of it; and second, never to fall into the trap of assuming that written output automatically or immediately leads to external rewards. Find other ways of sustaining your commitment to writing. Feeling that you have made a contribution; helping to explore a subject more successfully or more clearly than the literature has done to date; making a difference in the lives and the learning of your students can all be meaningful endorsers of your effective writing strategy.

'Flow'

The experience of flow refers generally to the intrinsically enjoyable experience of getting into the swing of writing and becoming so engaged that your thoughts, ideas and words start to flood out. Often, when academics are asked to identify what it is they like about writing, they talk about a range of experiences that are connected, we believe, to this important experience of flow. The fact that very many of them actually use this word is one indicator that the concept is an important and central one that relates to the pleasures of academic writing. But they also invoke a range of other connected ideas: they talk about how exciting it is when they've really got 'into' a writing task; they talk about the pleasure of 'getting lost' as opposed to the negative aspects that that experience sometimes conveys; they admit that it's difficult to get into a state of flow but also recognize that once they have achieved it, it feels exhilarating, exciting, creative and affirmative in a whole range of important ways.

Csikszentmihalyi (1990) captured a lot of his own research and work in the area of 'flow' by studying people involved in engaged action. He defines flow as the psychology of optimal experience, and shows us that there are features of the flow experience that define it and allow all sorts of positive benefits to accrue. We propose that by installing these features as much as possible into your own writing contexts, you can become a more frequent beneficiary of a sense of satisfaction, enjoyment and creativity associated with the positive aspects of writing in academia. Csikszentmihalyi studied thousands of people over a period of several years in order simply to identify the characteristics of certain experiences that make them inherently enjoyable. The framework he applies to the concept of flow or optimal experience can be installed more frequently into academic writing contexts – a proposition that is discussed in more detail later in this chapter.

What do academics dislike about writing?

When academics talk about the things they don't like about writing, a very different list emerges. This finding is rather Herzbergian in nature (in the organizational behaviour literature, Herzberg famously found that job-related 'satisfiers' are qualitatively different from job-related 'dissatisfiers' rather than there being just a presence or absence of a series of generic factors relevant both to dissatisfaction and satisfaction). When academics were asked 'what do you dislike about academic writing?', their answers tended to fit into at least one of the following five categories:

The feeling of negative surveillance and enforcement to which their writing is subjected

When talking about what they dislike about writing, academics often say that it is the feeling of *having* to write that sometimes interferes with the feeling of *wanting* to write. That people will review their writing in a critical and negative way is something that can make them feel intimidated about taking the first step, or indeed about building the confidence and momentum that they can feel when they do get into a flow of writing. Surveillance and enforcement are part of the academic realm that people associate with unpleasant, pressurized, judgemental aspects of writing.

A feeling of inertia or difficulty with getting started

Many academic writers talk about the agonies of just getting down to it. Getting started is often experienced as a difficult and unpleasant part of the process. Perhaps this is because writing, unlike other parts of our professional lives, is not scheduled and structured or driven by a predictable, externally defined timetable in the same way as, say, teaching, marking, and administration activities tend to be.

A feeling of getting stuck or being blocked, or difficulty in moving from one phase or type of writing to another

The experience of being 'blocked' is also something that academics talk frequently about. 'I just don't know what to do next'; 'the whole task feels so overwhelming'. These are common statements about writing that imply that there are obstacles, either real or imagined, that do stand in the way and prevent or delay our writing tasks. It is the feeling of being blocked that people say is unpleasant, and the things (as discussed above) that are enjoyable about writing generally represent solutions to or antidotes for those feelings of blockage.

A general sense of inadequacy about writing skills, processes and outputs

Confidence, or rather a lack of it, is often cited by academics as the rationale for not starting, or not continuing, to write. The academic world is one in which professional self-esteem and self-belief are sometimes under attack. If you operate in dysfunctionally competitive environments, there may be no one in the system willing to help you to believe in yourself and there may be those who actively undermine your sense of confidence even if you are doing an excellent job. All of this can contribute to a deflation and a diminishing of your motivation to write, perhaps even at times where your ability to make a meaningful contribution is at its highest. Of course, it's not just about confidence. Confidence may help you to get started or fuel your writing efforts, but you do also need to build skills, to practise and even to model your writing depending on the discipline within which you write. Many academics genuinely feel that they lack both the competence and the confidence to write in their area of expertise and these are among the common reasons why academic writing can be experienced as challenging and difficult.

Difficulties associated with finding one's own voice as an academic writer

Related to the issues of confidence and competence is that of academic voice. Many academic writers or academics who want to write say that one of the things that they dislike is this feeling of being somehow constrained in what they are trying to say. This is either because they feel they have something to say but don't possess the language to articulate it properly, or because the conventions of their academic discipline forbid them from writing freely, without constraint, in their own words. The issue of voice is articulated largely in two ways: not having an adequately articulate academic voice; or having a voice that is strangled and distorted by the requirements associated with the genres of one's discipline. Both of these concerns are associated with a dislike of writing in academia.

Overcoming the dislikes of academic writing requires us not necessarily to ignore them, as they are unlikely to go away. At least occasionally they may have to be encountered, addressed and tackled. Rather, it requires us to start with the things we like and to begin to feel that there are more positive things about the process than there are negative things.

The elements of enjoyment

According to Csikszentmihalyi (1990), there are eight conditions that prepare the ground for an experience to be enjoyable, intrinsically motivating or 'flow-like' in nature. Activities which involve flow are characterized by:

1 inherent challenge;
2 the fusion of action and awareness;
3 clear goals and feedback;
4 full concentration on the task;
5 some sense of control;
6 a feeling of effortlessness;
7 a lack of self-consciousness;
8 a lack of awareness of the passage of time.

Flow is that pleasurable 'getting lost' in a task or an activity that many of our colleagues have talked about when asked to identify the positive, enjoyable aspects of the academic writing process. It's an experience that makes you surprised when you look up at the clock and see that hours have passed; or alternatively when time 'stretches' or even stands still and when a lot can feel like it has happened, even in a few short minutes or seconds. Writing is hard and pleasureless when we're forever feeling distracted and pulled in all sorts of other directions, a feeling that prevents us from achieving the total focus that it sometimes takes for us to get our thoughts, ideas, structures, evidence and analyses down on paper.

Writing is a chore when we're writing into the dark without any opportunity to see how we're getting on or to get some kind of feedback about the quality of our efforts. Writing can feel like a pointless process if it either doesn't require us to challenge ourselves or if the goals we set ourselves are too high. Again, understanding the process of flow can help us to get a better understanding of the paradoxes of writing that we explored in Chapter 1, and to set up writing contexts that make it more likely we'll start to like, even to love, the process of writing within our academic worlds.

Creativity

While academic writing might feel formulaic and inherently lacking in creativity, we argue that just like the production of anything, it is essentially a creative process. Research on creativity shows that one of the characteristics of creative people is simply that they have a strong sense of themselves as being inherently creative (Barron and Harrington, 1981). This may sound like a tautology, but we think it is a meaningful observation. It may be that part of the reason why many academics do not write, do not make time and space for writing, or report that they dislike the writing process, is that they do not see themselves as creative people or as people with a creative mandate. This may be as much an issue of identity as it is of action. Perhaps if academics played or experimented with their identity and focused more on their creative selves, the cultures and structures of academia might tilt more in favour of creative expression and breakthroughs in a way that could benefit teachers, learners, researchers and writers from all disciplines.

Writing *is* a very creative process – all the more so as you target your writing at increasingly exacting audiences. It requires you to do something, to act, to put words on paper, to make sense, to structure, to analyse and to contribute. All of these requirements imply creativity. In making positive advances in your writing by getting started, you might benefit from reflecting on the essential characteristics of creativity:

Csikszentmihalyi also studied eminently creative people to see whether there were 'ingredients' associated with their behaviour that explained their successes and the impact that they had on the world. In summarizing his findings, this is what he said:

> If I had to express in one word what makes their personalities different from others, it's complexity. They show tendencies of thought and action that in most people are segregated. They contain contradictory extremes.

The management and encountering of paradox also emerges as an essential feature of a creative orientation to work and life. Csikszentmihalyi's research (1990) identifies paradoxes associated with creative people. Creative people alternately engage in intense levels of physical activity but also are able to switch off (or step back and retreat from their activities) by availing of quiet, restful time. They are clever and engaged with their areas of expertise, but not smug – often displaying an innocence and naïveté about aspects of their work that allow them to ask simple, revelatory questions that can get them closer to solving problems. Creative people bring strong discipline to what they do, but never in such a serious or humourless way that they cannot also inject playfulness and fun into their work. They combine imagination with reality, rebelliousness with conservatism, humility with pride, and passion with objectivity.

Other research on the personal characteristics of creative people (Barron and Harrington, 1981; Eckert and Stacey, 1998) has highlighted that creative individuals have a wide breadth of interests and a readiness to receive and absorb ideas from any angle or source. They are more likely to think in boundery-less ways about a topic, and are happy to 'borrow' important notions from fields of inquiry other than their own. They exercise autonomy and an independence of judgement, and are persistent in their willingness to 'resolve anomalies or to accommodate opposite or conflicting traits in one's self-concept' (Runco, 2004a: 661).

These paradoxical and complex features of creativity could be useful to consider as you embark on your own current and future writing ventures.

When you just don't know where to start – experimenting with different kinds of writing

We have found that in order to become a more productive academic writer, it can be worthwhile practising your writing skills in a range of different ways. There are different kinds of writing, not all of which can be defined as academic, but through them, you can nourish your fluency in ways that may ultimately help you to become more prolific in more academic realms.

At what point does your writing become 'academic'? What is the role (if any) of other 'kinds' of writing? Can you use less threatening or structured genres as important stepping-stones that might eventually lead you to produce an academic, published output? There are lots of different writing options. You don't always have to engage in the same kinds of writing and you don't always have to write according to a structured set of rules.

Experimenting with different kinds of writing may help you to gain more confidence and momentum. Not all of your writing has to be purely and perfectly academic, even if serious academic writing is your ultimate goal.

If your ultimate aim or task is to finish your PhD, or to write a book, or to get published in an internationally renowned, peer-reviewed journal in your discipline, you really can benefit from writing that looks and feels different from the structured language associated with those 'higher-order' goals of academic writing. There are other options for writing within your professional context, options that might help you to step forward in some way with your work, even when you're not feeling particularly clever or intellectual, even when you don't feel ready to produce 'respectable' academic work, even when you're wondering how the whole thing will turn out, or when you feel you could benefit from throwing your ideas around with interested colleagues.

Different types of writing, then, can act as stepping-stones to what might be your ultimate destination. They include random private scribblings, written interactions with other people about your ideas (emails, letters, even text messages), concrete collaboration with people interested in similar topics, and 'profiled' collaboration – all of these might lead to written outputs that get you closer to the goals associated with publication, even though some of them may not be defined as writing that is academic. The point is that nearly any kind of writing has the potential to provide foundations or raw material for a final fully formed academic piece.

Different types of writing

- **Random private**: a personal private method of capturing and recording insights, ideas, anxieties, triumphs.
- **Organized private**: a way of organizing and capturing ideas before developing and exploring them with others.
- **Interactive**: a way of communicating informally, brainstorming and discussing possibilities about your writing with others.
- **Concrete collaboration**: working papers within a professional group to develop themes and capture activities.
- **Profiled collaboration**: transmitting collaborative work to other audiences in written form.
- **High-level professional profiling**: producing published output in structured, conventional journals or publication targets.

So, as well as aiming for high-level academic journals, you can generate ideas and writing fuel by doing something as simple as keeping a diary, by carrying a notebook with you and recording ideas or insights as they strike you (see also Moore and Murphy, 2005), by using your professional experiences to write material and resources for colleagues such as 'how to' outlines, learning resource packs, case studies, manuals, textbooks, lecture notes, study notes, distance learning resources and so on. You can develop a confidence in your voice by targeting newspapers, or consider other ways of reaching more generic audiences. You can develop a more academic approach by contributing to colloquia and conferences and then use the resulting experiences and insights to transform and craft your ideas for even more specialist academic audiences. And you can use all of these activities to move closer towards the ultimate goals associated with the more academic aspects of your writing.

By considering these other kinds of writing, you can then position writing as a means rather than exclusively as an end. As Hjortshoj (2001) has suggested, anxieties about writing may come from seeing it as an end; and excitement about writing may come from seeing it as a means.

But in considering all of these different starting points for your writing, it is probably legitimate and pragmatic to ask: how much of these other kinds of writing actually 'count'? Perhaps in their own right, none of them do, when it comes to career development, tenure or promotion. But if you can use them as catalysts for your advance phase and as facilitators of your writing and your confidence, then they all count. If they enable you to create the conditions for producing more structured academic writing eventually (or even quite quickly) then they count very much.

The downside of advancing

Advancing, becoming actively engaged, making a start and gaining confidence are all important dimensions of writing, and in this chapter we have tried to help you to explore what these kinds of orientations might mean for you. But such engagement does not come without risks and potential problems. Developing a prolific, progressive orientation towards your writing can become both tiring and stressful, especially in a context where you also have to deliver on many other work and life responsibilities (Fisher, 1995; Doyle and Hind, 1998). If you engage only in writing that is unbridled by concerns associated with structure and genre, then even the most insightful proliferation of ideas may not yield positive outcomes or may not feed into a more structured, organized approach to your academic writing strategy. Without the checks and balances associated with revisiting, reconceptualizing, revising and reworking your writing, you may start to work in a vacuum, uninformed or untested by useful ideas that might be sitting on your doorstep if only you crept out once in a while to take a look. In becoming determined to advance your work, also guard against a sort of overconfident isolation (Blanton et al., 2001) that could be countered by stepping back – a phase of writing that we'll explore in more detail in Chapter 3.

How to get started and become creatively engaged with your academic writing – checklist and strategy

- See yourself as part of a conversation and decide to join the dialogue.
- Identify how you can engage with current issues or unanswered questions in a way that might catalyse a reaction.
- Encourage your students to read written work of yours and that of other authors.
- Respond positively to requests to talk about your work.
- Explore your motivation (see also chapter 9).
- Track the times in your writing when you're most likely to feel engaged and focused.
- Avoid unstructured proliferation of ideas – set up your ideas file and keep them relatively organized.
- Generate targets and outlines that will help to avoid unstructured, uncaptured garrulous approaches to writing.
- Find what really interests you, something you care about or an angle about which you can feel passionate.

- Check the extracts of your writing that you feel most proud of, and try to identify the features of the context in which you wrote it.
- Keep a writing diary that allows you to track the rhythms of your writing.
- Talk to trusted others about your writing and capture important or striking aspects of that conversation.
- Protect time for advancing your writing – don't listen to voices that say you don't know enough – maybe this is true, but you won't always know where the gaps are until you have generated some skeletal outline of where it is you want to go.

3

Retreating

Reviewing, revising, crafting and enhancing your writing

Introduction • Defining the retreat phase: reviewing and recharging • From advance to retreat • Retreating in order to rest • Retreating to get feedback from others • Exercises in retreating from your writing • Checklist and strategy for retreating from your writing • Summary

Introduction

This chapter presents the importance of retreating or stepping back from your academic writing. It provides guidance about how to prepare to engage in this less active, more reflective, objective, detached mode. We argue that this is an essential phase of the academic writing process. We show how academic writers can benefit from the deliberate adoption of a retreat strategy at various key stages in their writing. It will also highlight the importance of balancing regular and successive phases of progress and revision.

Defining the retreat phase: reviewing and recharging

Our own observations have highlighted three important dimensions of the retreat phase of academic writing. The first is the important need to relax and rest from writing tasks, a need that may be precipitated by some of the negative experiences that are associated with the advance phase of writing. Signals that you may be ready to retreat from your writing include such things as exhaustion, stress and other signs that active writing may have reached a point where any progress is gradually characterized by diminishing returns. The second dimension of the retreat phase is that of re-evaluation, an activity that necessarily requires revisiting, getting feedback and listening to other people's views on what you have written. Writing in academia, like most other writing, involves sending your message to readers. Part of the retreat phase involves listening to the views of people who are likely to be able to tell you a lot about your writing, give you insights that you may not have considered yourself, and equip you with big and small ideas to help you to develop and to enhance your work. The third dimension of the retreat phase is getting ready for another phase of advance. After you have rested and switched off; after you have sought, received and reflected on feedback; then you need to gear up again and prepare for the next stage of progress.

Retreating from your writing represents a change of gear and can involve a range of different dynamics: a rest phase after a period of active writing; the incubation of and reflection on ideas that have already been at least partly formed; the 'handing over' of your writing to someone else and allowing your writing to be viewed through another lens. Retreating or stepping back means stopping, resting, thinking, reflecting, re-evaluating, revising and re-orientating your writing. All of these may be important things to do in order to produce a publishable, coherent piece of work.

The importance of retreating reflects the need for you to be cautious about becoming so immersed or locked into your work that you can't cast a more objective eye over what you have done.

Some of the key practical advice in this chapter includes guidelines for handing your writing to someone else; listening to or reading feedback and achieving relaxation and detachment in the context of even the most stressful and demanding writing projects.

From advance to retreat

Even the most prolific and successful academic writers say that the momentum they achieve when writing is not direct or automatic. While they write, they experience periods of active progress, but they also encounter periods of delay, criticism and re-evaluation. Just as one aspect of your writing is characterized by a gratifying sense of progress, another, complementary phase requires you to stop, to reflect and to review. Much of this involves simply putting down your pen, or printing off a piece of writing and switching off your computer. Some inevitably involves criticism and reflection. Part of it involves planning and sketching out next steps that can be taken with the benefit of the reflection that a retreat phase allows.

Rewriting and revisiting one's writing is not an admission of failure, nor should it be a depressing raking over the coals of one's inadequacies. Implicit in much existing work on writing 'blocks' is the argument that once writers can get over the notion that reviewing and criticizing their own writing is not a negative statement on the work that they have done to date, then they have made a crucial breakthrough in their relationship with their writing tasks (Hull, 1985). Re-evaluating your writing, preferably after a period of rest and detachment, is a positive and almost definitely a necessary phase in all your writing projects (Zinsser, 1980; Levine, 2004). The willingness to do this simply recognizes that you are moving from one phase of writing to the next. You are not taking a retrograde step but a progressive one, one that will get you closer to your goal of completion successfully and with satisfaction.

In the writing sessions that we have observed as facilitators of academic writing, we are often struck by how quickly and fluently self-confessed non-writers or blocked writers start to write. When the conditions feel right for them, and when writers step forward and start to advance, ink really does come flowing from pens, keyboards tap furiously and feverishly, people forget about what time it is, lose themselves in their writing and are often amazed to discover that hours have passed since they last lifted their head from their tasks. Once people start to write freely in this way, it often seems like there's no stopping them.

After many of the freewriting sessions that we have run, academic writers report how surprised they were to discover that they had so much to say. As we explored in Chapter 2, freeing people up from the restricted conventions of academic writing proves, perhaps ironically, to be a very effective way of helping people to make real progress on academic writing tasks. The academics we have worked with demonstrate huge engagement and satisfaction when they are in this phase of active progress, learning to write in a way that sidelines their concerns about rhetoric, genre, spelling, structure, at least for a time, in order to get into a productive writing mode. But like all happy, productive phases in our lives, it can't last forever. Prolific production of text eventually slows. People start to re-read and reconsider what they have written. The voices of doubt and caution start to whisper. The need for direction, sequence and organization starts to become clear. This may be the signal that you are about to enter a different but equally important phase in the writing process. And you should try to see this as a positive thing, not as the indicator that everything is about to grind to an inexorable and permanent halt.

Slowing down is just as important as speeding up. When you are writing fluently and unselfconsciously, there will come a time when you need to take stock. When moving forward with your writing, the project can start to feel overwhelming and stressful. Worries also emerge about deadlines, your knowledge base, the legitimacy of your arguments, the 'acceptability' of what you have written, the robustness of your data or your assertions, the comprehensiveness of your frame of reference, the appropriateness of your influences and the relevance of the literature you have cited.

You may be able to address these questions more effectively and assiduously if you deliberately plan to enter a phase of retreat from your writing. It allows you to re-evaluate rather than abandon; to rework rather than reject. It can help you to engage in useful criticism of your work. Do you know enough to make a particular argument? Do you have enough data to deliver a particular assertion? Is your writing in its current form suitable for your target publications? While these questions can feel stressful and frustrating, perhaps they will feel less so if, from the beginning, you plan ahead of time to pause at some point and ask them. You can start to resent such considerations because they take you out of the more satisfying phase of flow in which everything was coming easily to you and you weren't worrying so much about the issues of rigour or quality. Before you address these considerations, then, the first thing that it is useful to do when retreating from your writing, is to do nothing at all, to relax and to switch off.

Retreating in order to rest

So, there does come a stage in academic writing tasks when constant, relentless engagement in your writing is simply unproductive. Working actively on your writing, or feeling it forever hanging over you, can create a semi-tolerable, but rather unpleasant life – one in which you are constantly vulnerable to being distracted from other important things in your life for the sake of your writing, always at risk of allowing your writing task to take over, always in danger of being drawn away from the present moment in which you might be relaxing, socializing, spending time with your family, or getting other things done at work or at home.

We encourage you to nurture the skill of switching off completely and to learn that just because you leave your writing for a while, doesn't mean that the words you have written are going to evaporate or that you will never be able to pick up the threads, or that the next time you start, you'll feel it will not be picking up where you left off, but starting all over again. Over-engaged writers do fear these things and, because of these fears, are often reluctant to stop once they've started, writing for long blocks of time in ways that are ultimately damaging and unhealthy for them (Boice, 1990). When asked why they do this, some of them do refer to the pleasure of flow and of getting lost in a writing task, as described in Chapter 2, but many of them report that they simply don't trust themselves to be able to come back to a writing task once they have left it.

Productive, successful writers, and those who derive more pleasure out of writing, are those writers who have found ways of planning and organizing their time in a way that creates balance between their writing and all the other important aspects of their lives. We need strategies for taking our breaks. It is not advisable just to get up and walk away, creating a Miss Havisham-style dusty desk left exactly as it was on the day you abandoned it. If you plan your retreat phase, it will be less an abandonment of your writing, and more a strategic regrouping of your energies, your perspectives and your motivation. Sometimes simply going to sleep can give you insights and ideas about your work (Wagner et al., 2004). Turk and Kirkman (1998) advise: 'try to leave [your writing] for a few days, or at least overnight . . . it is essential to make a conscious effort to step back from your work' (p. 41). Here is some more practical advice that you might benefit from when planning your rest periods.

Practical advice for taking breaks from your writing

1. Make your breaks complete

In order to function at their best, our brains need periods of intense and profound rest. The benefits of switching off are well documented (for example Jensen, 1995; Cooper, 2000; Schneider, 2003), and may be particularly important for those involved in academic writing tasks. In order to switch off completely from the task in which you are embroiled, you need to get some kind of closure from the active phase of writing. It might help to print off parts or all of what you have written and to have a quick read with a view to editing it at a later stage. Going through basic housekeeping rituals might make it easier for you to get some temporary distance from your task and to retreat from your active writing phase.

2. Make your breaks timed – know when your next writing period is going to be

Too often, writers are taken away from their writing tasks not having a firm idea about when they'll next get around to writing again. Having a writing schedule is a useful way of ensuring that you don't leave too much time between writing sessions. The psychology of knowing when you are going to revisit your writing before you take a break from it will allow you to plan in more concrete ways and give you a sense of continuity and optimism. Some of the discipline imposed by membership of a writers' group (see Chapter 7 for a detailed outline of the writers' group concept) can help to inject this sense of continuity in your writing, even when you're not doing it.

You may need to negotiate this time in quite assertive ways with all sorts of people in your life (see also Chapter 9). But once you do have a schedule, then you will be more deliberate about how much time you spend both with and away from your writing tasks. This will allow you to take breaks without feeling guilty or worried that you're turning your back on your writing completely.

3. Write a list of what needs to be done next before leaving your writing task

Before you stop writing, it's useful to sketch out a list of the things that you want to do next. It might be an outline, a list of words or some general ideas of steps and aspects that you would like to cover. It might be a plan of which sections of a particular outline you want to tackle next. Having a writing action plan means that, again, it will be easier to pick up where you left off. It is useful to end a particular writing session with a 5-minute freewriting exercise using a prompt like: 'The ideas that I want to write about next are . . .', or more specifically: 'at my next writing session I would like to . . .' The more specific you are about the writing tasks you want to return to, the easier it will be (Elbow and Belanoff, 2000; Murray, 2002). This is important when you're planning a period away from the task. It is unlikely that you have the power of perfect recall – it's easy to forget where you were. A planned list of next steps will jog your memory and reassure you that you do actually know where you are going. It will save you time and make it easier for you to take breaks when your energy is dipping and when you just need to go away and do something else.

4. Do something completely different: exercise, entertainment, socializing, meditating, massage, yoga, swimming

In order to make sure you really do take a proper break, it's worth planning to do something totally different than the activities that you usually engage in while writing. Avoid breaks that keep you sitting down, have you in front of a computer or involve tiring reading- or writing-related tasks. Watching television might seem like a break from writing, but it probably won't provide enough of a change of scene to stop you from being preoccupied with your task. Psychologists suggest that the best kinds of work-related breaks involve active, moderately challenging physical activities that keep you engaged and stop you from thinking about the tasks from which you are supposed to be getting a break.

5. Don't actively try to think about your writing project – but bring a notebook with you – just in case

While your breaks should be complete and utterly diverting, don't ban your brain from its inevitable ability to gain important insights about your writing while you are away from your task. Often it is at the very time you are resting that the best ideas pop into your head – so let that happen, just don't force it to. If you do have a brainwave while relaxing, make a note of it. Keep your 'ideas' notebook with you even when you're not working, so that any interesting insights that might strike you won't go to waste, and later on you can exploit them more deliberately during your next dedicated writing session. Allow your ideas to marinate so that the content will be tender and easier to tackle on your return.

Retreating to get feedback from others

At least as important as rest and detachment is the dimension of retreat that involves getting feedback from others. Boice (1982) once suggested that academics who don't write choose not to do so because of such things as negative early experiences, a tendency towards perfectionism or even grandiosity and anxiety associated with evaluation. As you saw in Chapter 2, we have found similar issues invoked in our own explorations about what people dislike about academic writing. Most of these writing prohibitors are linked, at least in some way, to the issue of feedback.

Being ready to revise requires the ability to 'decentre' and allow yourself to see your work through the eyes of others (Kroll, 1978; Bradford, 1983). Once you give your writing to someone to read, you take the control out of your hands and you give it to someone else. It is both stepping back and letting go. It is allowing someone else to start to play a role.

The psychology of negative feedback

Negative feedback is the conundrum of feedback. Few beliefs are more widely accepted by psychologists, managers, educators, and others concerned with human performance than the belief that people need to receive feedback about how well they are performing their tasks . . . Yet in spite of the best intentions to stimulate performance improvement with negative feedback, it rarely works that way; all too often negative feedback produces the opposite effect.

(Ilgen and Davis, 2000: 551)

When people are exposed to information that is uncomfortable or threatening to them, they tend to deny, distort, ignore or avoid it (Festinger, 1958). Academic writers are constantly risking what psychologists call cognitively dissonant experiences, particularly when they submit their work for review and criticism to international, peer-reviewed journals or to uncompromising editors. On the one hand, they are told that their tenure or progression within academia depends on their ability to publish their work, while on the other, receiving any negative perspectives on their work can make them feel like they are further away than ever from their writing and publishing goals. These two conflicting experiences often lead academics to abandon projects that are actually full of promise or to avoid situations in which they will receive any negative feedback about their work whatsoever. After several bouts of criticism or rejection, many of them start to feel that not working on a writing task at all might be preferable. Negative feedback, even if logically full of potential utility and insightful lessons about your performance, often produces the opposite of its desired effect. Instead of a determination to improve, people withdraw, dejected and discouraged. Instead of an urge to gain insights about the general and specific ways in which a piece of writing falls short of the mark, people avert their eyes from the criticism, some not even allowing themselves see it, let alone learn lessons that could help them use it.

The psychology of positive feedback

Just as it is difficult to encounter negative feedback about your work, it's also very pleasant to hear positive things. This is all the more the case if such feedback comes from authoritative sources or from those whose opinion you respect. Make sure you pay attention to the lessons that positive feedback can contain. It's just as important to analyse what's good about your writing as it is to get a reasonable picture about what it is about it that needs improvement or change. Interrogate the positive perspectives as assiduously as you analyse the negative ones. This will be important as your writing strategy unfolds. Be careful that positive feedback does not lead to arrogance or complacency. Make sure that you make use of the positive feedback you receive by focusing carefully on exactly what it is that makes a particular piece of writing so good. If you do this, then it is likely that you'll learn both from your writing successes as well as your writing failures and be equipped as much by positive as by negative perspectives on your writing.

Potential blocks to effective feedback

If writers don't look for feedback at all, they miss out on important opportunities to improve their work

Many of the academic writers we have worked with say that it sometimes feels hard to trust people to read their work in progress. They prefer to work privately or even secretly, fearing that if they do share their work, they'll be risking ridicule, jealousy or bad advice. Even when trust levels are high, writers often assume that writing is a purely solitary task, one that does not involve or require interaction with other people. But we believe that writing is better conceived of as both iterative and interactive. While it may be important to contain and keep your writing private in the early stages, getting feedback that is constructive and healthy generally creates opportunities for improving written work.

This opportunity might still not be enough of a motivation for you to seek it out, though. A lot of academic writers say that when someone points out possible new avenues for their writing, or gaps that they may need to fill with further research and investigation, it creates more, not less, stress for them. Many of them say things like: 'I don't care what's wrong with it, I just need to get it finished', or 'No matter what you tell me about this, I can't imagine ever wanting to do any more work on it.' These reactions are common and normal in academia. If you've ever experienced perspectives like this on your work, we suggest that stepping back by getting feedback is even more important than you might have imagined. Needing to stay in control of their writing, even when other people are reading and commenting on it, is something that writers often report. You can get feedback while also feeling and staying in control.

If writers wait until they are completely committed to a finalized piece of writing before looking for feedback, then it may be harder for them to face the prospect of making any changes at all

The early, fluid, flexible stages of a writing project are often ideal times to get feedback from others about what you're doing. Conversely, when you have crossed every 't' and dotted every 'i', when you have drafted and redrafted your writing, polished and finalized it without reference to the views or inputs of anyone else, it can be much more difficult to countenance changing it or to incorporate even the most useful inputs from others. So, it may be that early drafts are the easiest to get advice on. Besides, you are likely to be able to be less defensive if you haven't worked day and night to make it as good as you feel it can be before showing it to someone else.

If writers don't tell advisers about the kind of feedback they need to help them keep writing, the feedback they do get might be more damaging than beneficial

Elbow and Belanoff (2000) suggest that people should be much more pointed when asking for feedback. Based on their experiences and research with writers, they recommend that you become much more deliberate about managing the feedback process. Don't just hand your drafts nervously to someone and say something vague like: 'tell me what you think'. They suggest, for example, that anyone you give your writing to should be fully briefed about the stage of writing that you are at, how much and what kind of feedback you have already received and from whom, what kind of advice you would find most useful at this stage in the project. They suggest that there are many different kinds of sharing and feedback that you can receive, and provide a list of options that are summarized at the end of this chapter.

By asking your readers for specific kinds of feedback, you suddenly become more 'in charge' of the feedback you receive, and as a result, are more likely to feel a sense of control rather than desperate helplessness that writers often talk about when they have 'released' their work to other people.

If writers are afraid of feedback, they may ignore, distort or deny its validity

Nobody likes to hear negative comments about themselves or their work. On the one hand, logic would suggest that if you want to reach a particular goal, then you should find any perspectives or information about your performance very useful. The truth is that for academic writers, the fear of negative feedback is very strong. It is often the one thing that causes many academic writers to avoid writing altogether, or to make much slower progress than might otherwise be the case. Kluger and DeNisi (1996) have argued that in general terms critical feedback may be necessary to help you to improve and progress on any task, but it can also have a prohibitive impact on your motivation and momentum. Again, this reinforces the importance of being aware and staying in charge of the kinds of feedback you need to help you progress.

If writers don't analyse feedback calmly and objectively, they may find it harder to improve their writing and chances of publication

Academic writers don't tend to get themselves into a deliberate frame of mind when listening to or reading feedback on their work. They report receiving and reading rejection letters or reviewers' comments in hurried, harried ways during busy times of the year. Most feedback, even the friendliest kind, indicates possibilities for more, not less, work – something that people are sometimes not even ready to countenance while rushing between meetings and lectures. And so what emerges in their writing is characterized by 'writer's block', demotivation, disaffection and inactivity. The one activity that can be so transformative, that can facilitate learning and knowledge creation, that can yield so much self-efficacy and pride in one's work can be a destructive force in academic career or professional development. This happens for many, many academics in almost all institutions. We estimate, based on our own interactions with academics around the world, that this kind of withdrawal is a global phenomenon. But, it is one that we think can be addressed by encouraging people to train themselves to allocate time to their feedback, and to become deliberately calmer and more objective about advice they receive. Doing this could help you to develop robust and questioning writing strategies.

Functional approaches to getting feedback on your writing

1. Understanding the importance of audience

> What writers need is *an audience*: a thoughtful, interested audience. In the long run, you will learn most about writing from feeling the *presence of interested readers* – like feeling the weight of a fish at the end of the line.
>
> (Elbow and Belanoff, 2000: 508)

Our experience also supports Elbow and Belanoff's claim that interested readers are one of a writer's greatest assets. However, Grant and Knowles (2000) evocatively talk about writers holding their work to their chests protectively claiming 'it's not ready, I can't show it to anyone, it's not perfect'. It is very common for writers to be reluctant to show their work to anyone at all. That is, until it is too late to receive any useful advice about the text that they have produced. Good, productive, effective writers either don't experience this common human tendency or have found a way to overcome it.

A note on humility in writing

I think that one needs a great deal of humility to be a writer.
So it was with my father, who was a blacksmith and wrote tragedies, and did not value his writing of tragedies more highly than his shoeing of horses. Rather the contrary: when he was shoeing horses, he would never let anyone say to him, 'no, not like that . . . like this. You've done it all wrong.' He would look up with his blue eyes and smile or laugh; and he would shake his head. But when he was writing . . . he listened to what anyone said to him, and did not shake his head but agreed with them. He was very humble about his writing; he said that everyone had a hand in it; he tried for love of his writing, to be humble and to learn from others in every field.

(Vittorini, 1959)

The truth is, that anyone who is prepared to read drafts of your work should be treasured and availed of as often as possible once the very early fragile stage has been navigated. The earlier you are able show your work to others, the sooner you'll get other perspectives, be able to clarify what's not clear, be able to structure what seems unstructured, be able to set about correcting what seems incorrect, be able to 'round out' your writing in a way that benefits from the intelligent views, insights and inputs of other people. In order to benefit from the advice of others, there is a need to detach oneself somewhat from one's work, to be prepared to cast a critical eye on it so that the criticism of others does not come as a shock, and that you don't go into 'defensive mode', a place in which it is difficult to hear or to respond to even mildly negative views or questions that have been provided by someone else.

2. The beauty of criticism

By giving you their views, critical readers demonstrate to you that they have paid attention to your writing. Criticism is an indicator of engagement, active interest and a willingness to develop and respond to what you have already written. It contains seeds of new ideas, challenges to old ones and secrets to enhancing your writing. And that is informative, even if you decide for the time being to do nothing about it. If you do, criticism helps you to clarify the stances you have taken in your writing, and enhance the authority, rigour, robustness and professionalism of your writing. Good criticism can help you develop a writing project and ensure that it will progress into an interesting, effective, influential, publishable piece of work. Responding positively to criticism can ultimately lead you to discover satisfying and effective forms of your own writing.

3. The utility of receptivity: becoming a receptive listener

You may find it particularly helpful to reflect carefully on how, at what stage and with whom you should share your work. Once you have made that decision, you can help to manage the process of sharing your work by paying attention, and listening carefully and respectfully. By all means also question the basis of the feedback – not to challenge it, but rather to find out more about what the valuable reader is thinking. When you give your work to someone to read, it's worth keeping in mind that your readers have a right to their reactions. If they have taken the trouble to read your work carefully and thoughtfully, then you are at least obliged to allow them to decide what they think themselves. Arguing with readers or assuming they haven't understood is not very useful. What is much more useful is listening carefully to what they are saying and trying hard to understand whether what they have said can be used to help improve what you have written. Telling your reader that they don't understand something, or even getting shirty with them about any negative things they have to say, is much less useful than asking them to explain in more detail why they have reacted in the way that they have. Achieving a reflective orientation allows you to adopt a more objective stance so that you are not hurt, annoyed or insulted by critical readers, but energized and motivated by them.

4. Staying in charge

While empowering your critical reader, it is also important not to become disempowered yourself. It is important to feel active, in charge and relaxed. No matter what other people say, this is still your writing and only you ultimately must decide what (or what not) to do with it. Don't be subservient or helpless. You can decide what kind of feedback, if any, you need and you can choose what you want to do with it (Elbow, 1973; Turk and Kirkman, 1998).

So, in stepping back from your work, it is important to ask for what you want and then allow your critical reader to provide it. Listening carefully, curiously and undefensively will help you to make the most of the feedback you get. The exercise section at the end of this chapter provides you with a series of feedback options that you might consider looking for at different stages in your writing process. The important thing to remember is that you can choose the kinds of feedback you would like to get and you can maintain control over how you respond.

5. A focus on professional development and learning

Some of the things that may distinguish regular, successful academic writers from their less productive counterparts are: a willingness to learn from the perspectives of others, a curiosity about any comments that relate to their writing and a determination to integrate these perspectives into their subsequent writing strategies (Faigley and Witte, 1981; Zerubavel, 1999). By adopting these strategies yourself, you will be more likely to use all feedback in positive and professionally helpful ways.

6. Letting other people play a role in your writing

Furthermore, engaging in a search for feedback allows you to breathe a sigh of relief no matter what happens, because you create a stage in your writing project in which suddenly the ball is in someone else's court. Someone else undertakes to do something with what you have done, to say something about it, to subject it to some analysis or to suggest ways in which it can be improved. This simply allows you to sit back quietly for a while and to listen carefully to perspectives on your work. Be calm and reflective about what other people say. Feedback will not always be useful, but it is much more likely to be useful if you listen to it and reflect on what it means for your writing strategy.

7. Coping with unhelpful or destructive feedback

Sometimes, even when you seek out useful feedback, you get responses that may not only be unhelpful, but that create obstructions and blocks in your writing progress. There is no guarantee that the feedback you get won't at least occasionally be unclear, inaccurate, incomprehensible or difficult to respond to. Many academic writers can tell you about intemperate, insulting and unhelpful feedback that still sometimes comes from anonymous reviewers of international journals. You should be aware that not all analysers of your work will be motivated to encourage you to improve it, and not all of them will be positive enough to give you feedback that you can do something about. This makes it all the more useful to have positive writing partnerships in your professional life. The following section provides some preliminary advice about setting up supportive writing partnerships. You can also read about more detailed, contextualized approaches to doing this in Part II of this book.

Setting up writing partnerships and some guidelines for providing effective feedback

Setting up an effective writing partnership involves finding someone who is prepared to spend time getting involved in thoughtful dialogue about your writing. You're most likely to be able to do this if you offer to read someone else's work in return for them reading yours. In setting up a partnership like this, as well as reflecting on how best to respond to feedback you'll receive, it is also worth agreeing ground rules for giving feedback. It might be worth integrating the following feedback guidelines into your writing partnerships:

- Give feedback that you think will facilitate improvement (Ilgen and Davis, 2000).
- As well as identifying aspects of the writing that could be strengthened, point out strengths that already exist. Be honest and specific with both your positive and negative comments.
- Ask the writer to be specific about the kind of feedback they would find most useful and also to specify the stage of development of the writing (Elbow and Belanoff, 2000).
- Differentiate between higher-order and lower-order concerns (Bean, 2001). Higher-order concerns could include whether the writing addresses key questions, is argued in sound and justified ways or is well organized and clear. Lower-order concerns include such issues as stylistic choices, forms of expression, grammar, punctuation, spelling and layout.
- Always write/give feedback in a way that respects the person whose work you are commenting on, and that recognizes how your feedback is likely to make them feel (Goleman, 1995).

Exercises in retreating from your writing

This chapter has explored how important it is to see your academic writing from perspectives other than your own, but also of not being overwhelmed or paralysed by the feedback you receive. These exercises provide some practical strategies to help you to strike that important balance.

Exercise 1: Contextualizing your work to enhance the feedback process

When working with a writing mentor or partner, try contextualizing your work. Prompts that might be useful in initiating feedback might sound like this:

- 'Before you give me feedback on this piece, this is what you need to know': e.g. the evolution and stage of my writing (first draft, redraft, revisited after a long time, unstructured, polished).
- 'These are the reasons I wrote this piece.'
- 'I have received feedback about a previous draft that advised me to . . . and these are the ways in which I have tried to integrate that advice.'

Exercise 2: Deciding on the feedback you want

(Adapted from Elbow and Belanoff, 2000)

You can ask your feedback givers to provide you with different kinds of feedback. Select a piece of writing that you are currently working on, and reflect on which of the following feedback instructions would be most useful for you to give your mentor in the interests of progressing this work:

1 **Highlight the essential, central messages in my writing**
   Ask readers to identify what they think is the most important, central statement in your writing. If your readers do this, it will be satisfying if the centre of gravity that they have identified is the same as you intended, and interesting if they identify something different.

2 **Invite me to elaborate on particular aspects of my writing**
   Ask readers to identify what they want to hear more about. This can trigger your capacity to elaborate and build on the most interesting aspects of your work.

3 **Tell me what you know/think/feel about the topic**
   Even if they are not experts in your discipline, the knowledge bases, ideas and opinions of trusted others might help to uncover new angles or lenses through which to view and develop your writing.

4 **Tell me how much 'voice' you hear in my writing**
If your writing mentors are confused by this question, then perhaps ask them to tell you if they would know that it was you who wrote these words. This can help you to explore the extent to which you are developing an independent, confident style in your writing. As Elbow and Belanoff put it: 'When people describe the voice they hear in writing, they often get to the subtle but important matters of language and approach' (2000: 513).

5 **Be my writing champion**
Ask your critical reader to identify only the things about your writing that they think are good. This is a useful instruction to give someone at times when you're feeling fragile and tentative about your work. Asking someone to tell you what they think is good can boost your confidence at times when you need it. You can help your reader to do this for you by asking them to do things like build on, develop or brainstorm aspects of your work.

6 **Be my devil's advocate**
Ask your critical reader to identify only those things about your work that they think are weak or need more attention. You might do this at times when you're feeling robust and confident by encouraging your reader to doubt, question, 'needle', even tease you about your writing. This could give you some valuable routes to enhancing what is already good or to reconsidering aspects of your writing that require further attention.

7 **Summarize my writing**
Ask your critical reader to take a piece of your writing and sketch out a summary or outline of it. This can be very helpful if you feel your writing is messy or unstructured, and can facilitate your subsequent efforts to tidy, craft and clarify your work.

8 **Give me specific feedback on aspects of my writing (criterion-based feedback)**
Direct your critical readers to specific criteria that are concerning you. It can be particularly useful to get criterion-based feedback when you are producing later drafts of your work. Specific criterion-related questions could include: Is this clear enough? Is my writing simple enough to convey these central ideas? Is this section too short/too long? Do you feel I've justified my assertions in this section? Could you read this piece with a view to picking up misspellings, typos or grammatical mistakes?

Checklist and strategy for retreating from your writing

- Plan to take regular breaks from your writing, especially at times when you have made a lot of active or intense progress.
- Be vigilant for signs that you may need to start stepping back from your work. These signs might include: slowing down of your writing momentum, a lack of structure, a sense of repetitiveness, uncertainty or fatigue.
- Practise switching off. Stop thinking about your writing. Try to leave it behind and not brood or mull over it during these switch-off times.
- Get used to showing your work to other people. If you find this difficult, start with small pieces of your writing, and choose to show it to someone you really trust to be sensitive but also honest about their reactions.
- Try to decide on what kind of feedback will be most likely to help you make progress on your work, and then ask for it.
- Analyse positive feedback on your writing as assiduously as you analyse negative feedback.
- In assimilating feedback, take notes and plan the ways in which you are going to start re-engaging with your work with the benefit of the advice and inputs on your writing.

Summary

This chapter emphasized the necessity of refocusing and sharpening one's work. Retreating can be triggered by difficult experiences within our academic careers – experiences that also risk leading to writer's block or other forms of professional paralysis. Such experiences include receiving a negative peer review of a paper, a supervisor's critique, or others' critical questioning of the merits or rationale underpinning one's work. We hope that this chapter helped you to think about how you can treat such experiences as catalysts, as opportunities for regrouping, as facilitators for reflection, and essentially as ways of enhancing your academic writing.

Our analysis of writers in retreat phase shows that there are three dimensions to this phase of the writing process. The first involves rest and relaxation and requires you simply to switch off for a period of time and to stop thinking about or doing writing. This disengagement is useful, nourishing and healthy.

The second dimension of retreat involves revisiting and re-evaluating – activities that are best achieved with input from other people and that allow you to look at your writing in different ways, from different critical standpoints, with a view to improving it.

The third dimension is re-engagement, where you start actively to improve your work, and get re-energized to develop it, moving again into a phase of active progress. And so the iterative cycle of writing continues, as does your capacity to improve and to enhance both the processes you use to write and the content of the text that you produce.

Just as it may be important for you to contain your writing and, at the early, fragile stages to protect it from the eyes of critical others (Cameron, 1999), it is also important to get your writing to a point where you are prepared to incorporate the views of others.

If you become more deliberate about, and accustomed to, retreating, you can start to make significant and potentially transformative steps in the enhancement of your academic writing.

4

Disciplinarity in academic writing

Analysing genre in your discipline • Analysing journal abstracts • Analysing journals: what can it tell you about disciplinarity? • Developing your own 'voice' • Checklist

Disciplinarity is constructed, in a sense, by published writing in your discipline, and your sense of disciplinarity is shaped by your understanding not only of research, but also of how research is presented in journals and, more importantly, how the case for 'contribution' to the discipline is constructed in writing.

Disciplinarity is often held up as one of the most important features of academic study, research and writing. This suggests that, if you want to write within a specific discipline, you need to establish what constitutes 'disciplinarity' in your area and, more specifically, how that is represented in published academic writing in your field at this time. This approach to disciplinarity is rhetorical, in the sense that it involves analysing features of texts and considering the audiences and purposes of academic writing.

Writing in a discipline undoubtedly means using certain rhetorical features, and as writers we have to assimilate those features into our thinking and writing. This may seem like a process of learning and/or adapting. We assume that academics are familiar with a range of journals, but few have conducted the type of detailed analysis featured in this chapter.

If this idea is new to you, one implication may be that your understanding of academic writing in your discipline would benefit from more detailed analysis of published writing than you currently do. Our analyses provide an indication of the type of work you can – and perhaps should – do, particularly for journals you intend to target.

This chapter explores the importance of understanding the academic discipline within which you work and write. We describe how disciplinarity can be understood in terms of the features of academic writing that currently appear in published form in your discipline. We identify both common and distinctive features of academic writing published in a selection of journals and propose specific ways in which you can deepen your knowledge of these features so as to incorporate them into your academic writing, as appropriate.

Towards the end of the chapter, we revisit the issue of maintaining your own voice within your academic writing.

Analysing genre in your discipline

The purpose of this section is to demonstrate that analysis of published writing can reveal features of a discipline, that these features may be varied – presenting you with a range of options for your writing – and that this range is not infinite. You can carefully specify the range for each journal. We suggest that you can, in spite of variation between and within journals, make generalizations about writing in your discipline.

The aim of analysis of published papers is to identify characteristics of academic writing in the sub-set of a discipline represented by any given journal. While you may wonder what you can learn from analysis of journals in disciplines other than your own, and while we would not argue against discipline-specific analysis, you may find that you can learn generic lessons from looking at how academic writing is produced in other disciplines.

This analytical process may seem to involve retreating from your own writing in order to analyse others'. This does not mean that you have to stop writing; but you may find that you have to develop new strategies – described elsewhere in this book – for continuing to write while you are defining the requirements of specific journals. Ultimately, this analysis should help you to advance in your own writing in a way that is likely to be judged appropriate in a specific context.

Some writers fear that they will lose momentum if they stop to analyse, and some find the study of published papers leaves them feeling intimidated, if the standards are very high, or disillusioned, if the standards are lower than they expected. These reactions reveal authors' expectations – as will yours – and lead to a realization that some adjustment of expectations might be helpful. It may be difficult to achieve this working on your own, and this is an area that writers' groups and writing 'buddies' or mentors can help you work through (see Chapter 7).

It has been argued that the subject of our analysis should be a 'personal corpus' of our own writing. Such analysis would allow us to establish the discourse features of our individual 'textual profile' (Coniam, 2004: 55). Using this approach, you could establish which features you currently use most in your writing – for example, 'How much do you hedge or boost? How do you use directives? How much nominalization is there in your writing? What tense do you write in?' (Coniam, 2004: 55).

That is not the approach we take in this chapter, since we assume that rather than forming one profile, academic writing requires you to alter your writing for specific contexts – you already do – and that you will write in different ways for different journals – perhaps you already do that too – but that there is value in defining the expectations of each journal – through analysis, and even in moving across disciplines in developing your options and skills as a writer. We argue that it should not be a matter of 'What tense do you write in?' (Coniam, 2004: 55), but which tense is considered appropriate and is therefore, in a sense, required, for your target journal?

Once you have addressed a journal's requirements, you can move on to consider the extent to which you feel willing or able to use features of the discourse that occur in published papers. You can assess how much room for manoeuvre you have – how free will you be to challenge the dominant norms and forms, not just in journals in general, but in specific journals? What would be the benefit of doing so – to you, your work, to the readers of the journal and to other researchers?

You may, nevertheless, find that you do begin to 'study' your own writing. You may find yourself comparing a published author's writing with your own, pondering perhaps how you would have written about the subject. While this is not the same as developing your 'textual profile', you may find yourself becoming more aware of your preferences, habits and values in writing. You may already know that you like certain expressions and dislike others, for example, or that you admire papers that seem to 'flow' without the need for linking words, or that you dislike papers that use personal pronouns.

In discussions with academics, we frequently find that it is difficult to stop academic writers evaluating published papers according to their own criteria – even when we ask them not to – and to analyse them instead. There is, of course, nothing wrong with judging published papers, but the purpose of analysis – as opposed to evaluation – is to work out how papers are put together.

Your 'take' on these issues will, to some extent, be determined by the type of research or scholarship you do, or by the methods or approaches you use, or perhaps by your research philosophy. Equally important, however, is your choice about how you want to write about your work, which aspects you want to emphasize and which elements you judge to be most interesting and potentially valuable to your peers. These choices are unlikely to be 'free'. You may have to make adjustments to your preferred structure or style in order to present your research in a way that is currently acceptable to the research community. You can begin to define what is 'acceptable' by analysing what journals have 'accepted'.

This is not to say that editors and reviewers consciously sit down with a set of characteristics as they select papers for review and publication. There is currently insufficient data on precisely what they do, but we can assume that the papers they choose to publish have features that are valued, both in the research and the writing.

You can begin your analysis of published papers by focusing on specific characteristics:

• structure;
• statement claiming 'contribution';
• case made for sufficiency of evidence for contribution.

Other features merit analysis, including the use and placing of definitions, contextualization of the work, inclusion of counter-arguments, establishing authority, referencing style and so on. You can draw up your own list, and reading this chapter will help you develop your initial checklist and analytical process. Building on what you already know, you can develop a critical understanding of the conventions of your discipline.

You may, in the course of your reading and your own analysis, form the view that there are both generic features of academic writing and features of specific disciplines. It might be helpful if you could define and illustrate these. Consider whether specific journals, with their specific agendas, and types of writing, can be seen as sub-genres.

This is not to say that the papers published in any journal are either identical or uniform – for they clearly are not – but the purpose is to show that, while any issue of any journal will have a range of papers, that range is not infinite and, therefore, the range of writers' options is limited. The broader purpose, beyond this analysis in our chapter, is to give you a framework for continuing this type of scrutiny of journals in your discipline. This is probably your most important follow-up task for this chapter. One outcome may be that you draw up a 'profile' of your target journals. Some journals have a wide range of papers, and others a relatively narrow range. In any event your journal profiles will consist of options.

The next section of this chapter is a guide for the level of analysis that you can do on your target journals. The following analyses show how you can examine rhetorical strategies used in published papers in your discipline. We selected an issue of the journal *Cognitive Science* because it included both scientific and social science approaches, and we thought this would appeal to a wider audience. We analysed all five abstracts published in one issue. As you scan these five pieces, you will see the range of subject matter, including computational models, heuristics, motor learning, perceptual systems and the discipline of cognitive science itself, often combining empirical and theoretical arguments and contributions.

The abstracts vary in length. Titles take different forms, although the majority identify both the subject and type of work conducted. Following this initial impression of variety, there are other questions you can ask in order to begin a more detailed analysis. For example, the two most important questions concern how problems are identified and what constitutes a contribution. Both of these steps, in the context of an academic argument, can be performed in many different ways, and it can be helpful to define which ones are currently used in your target journals.

Analysing journal abstracts

- How is the rationale/problematic established?
- As far as you can tell from the abstract, how is the paper structured?
- How is methodology defined and justified?
- How is contribution 'branded'?

By 'branded' in the last point we mean, what type of contribution is offered, and how is the value of that type articulated? What kind of case is made for that type of contribution? (See our commentary on example 3 below.)

You can get signals about how the whole paper is structured from the abstract, and this can help you to structure your own papers. Alternatively, if you are writing for a journal that does not include the content of the whole paper in abstracts, then you are likely to have to produce that type. A third possibility is that both options are available – both abstracts that take the form of 'the whole paper in miniature' and those that function as introductions to the paper – and you will have to make a choice. This choice might be influenced by the type of research you have done, or by the association of one type of abstract, in your target journal, with that type of work.

The principle we articulate here is that, at every point in your analysis, you can – and perhaps should – consider whether you can produce the types of argument that you see in your target journal. Of course, if you feel that what is being published in your target journal is just too far removed from the research you do and how you want to write about it, then you may have to find another journal to send your work to, or make a case for challenging the current conventions in the journal. This may mean explicitly making a case for doing so, articulating why you think this is a strength and defining what you add by writing in this way. This can be stimulating for writers and readers alike, but you might want to rehearse your idea, briefly, with the journal editor.

In the following analysis we highlight, in bold, what we think are the key points in the argument and provide a commentary on the way in which the argument has been put together. The purpose is to demonstrate the level of analysis that you can do on your own target journals. In discussions of such analyses with academics, we find that there can be a range of reactions, and we include some of these in our commentary.

Journal abstract – example 1

Working memory resources are needed for processing and maintenance of information during cognitive tasks. Many models have been developed to capture the effects of limited *working memory* resources on performance. **However, most of these** models **do not account for** the finding that different individuals show different sensitivities to working memory demands, and **none** of the models **predicts** individual subjects' patterns of performance. **We propose a** computational **model** that accounts for differences in working memory capacity in terms of a quantity called *source activation*, which is used to maintain goal-relevant information in an available state. **We apply this model to** capture the working memory effects of *individual* subjects at a fine level of detail across two experiments. **This**, we argue, **strengthens** the interpretation of source activation as *working memory* capacity.

(Daily et al., 2001: 315)

The opening sentence of this abstract identifies the field of study, making a general, relatively uncontentious statement about it. The second sentence identifies an approach to that field, and the third defines the gap: as soon as you see the word 'however' you know that there is a shift, in this case from what has been done to what still needs to be done. Immediately, the authors 'propose' an alternative. Using the word 'propose' makes the purpose, and perhaps scope, of their paper explicit. There is no ambiguity.

The proportions of the abstract, up to this point, are also interesting: almost half is about the context of the work, the other half is about the work they did. The use of the term 'model' – early in the second sentence, in the third sentence, twice, and early in the fourth – makes direct links between phases in this 'story' and makes its logic clear. The technique of using a key, linking word early in several sentences works to make connections between sentences very clear, making the writing 'flow', a quality many academics say they seek.

However, some academics say they find this type of repetition irritating. If that is your reaction, perhaps this option for establishing links and coherence would not be available to you, even if you were targeting this journal – although other options are available here – or it may mean that you should review your thinking: there is nothing 'wrong' about this use of repetition, although some academics say they have learned that it is, if not exactly wrong, then poor style. They feel they should use variety rather than repetition.

Yet repetition is an effective linking strategy, particularly used in this way and at this point in a paper. Moreover, in any discipline, key terms will be used – and must be used – throughout papers, perhaps even more irritatingly to those who are averse to this style of writing. In this instance, it is difficult to make a case for avoiding this type of repetition. Why would you change a key term, a term that by definition you have to use frequently, just for the sake of variation?

Finally, the authors of this abstract define their contribution in their last sentence. The words in bold show the direct, explicit link between the third sentence – defining a problem – with the closing sentence – providing a solution.

To what extent could you use this abstract as a model, if you were writing for this journal? Your answer to this question might depend on the type of research you do, but it might also be possible to map your writing over this model:

- X . . . is/are needed for . . .
- Many models/approaches have been developed to . . .
- However, none of these accounts for/can predict/tell us about . . .
- We/This paper proposes a . . . that accounts for/predicts/provides information on . . .
- We apply this model/This model is applied/This paper describes the application . . .
- We argue that this/This strengthens the interpretation of/approach to . . .

This is not to say that you can plagiarize other people's writing – for clearly you must not – but it points out what might be considered as the underlying deep structure of academic writing. It may be, in other words, that the structure of this paper could be a model for other papers, for other journals and for other disciplines.

However, in the context of this analysis, there are four other possibilities, the next using a different structure for a more theoretical type of work.

Journal abstract – example 2

The work presented here investigates the process by which one group of individuals solves the problem of detecting deceptions created by other agents. A field experiment was conducted in which twenty-four auditors (partners in international public accounting firms) were asked to review four cases describing real companies that, unknown to the auditors, had perpetrated financial frauds. While many of the auditors failed to detect the manipulations in the cases, a small number of auditors were consistently successful. . . . We explain failure to detect deception by means of perturbations (bugs) in the domain knowledge of accounting needed to apply these heuristics to the specific context of financial statement fraud. **We test our theory by** showing that a computational model of fraud detection that employs the proposed heuristics successfully detects frauds in the cases given to the auditors in the four cases. **We then modify the model** by introducing perturbations based on the errors made by each of the auditors in the four cases. **The resulting models account for** 84 of the 96 observations . . . in our data.

(Johnson et al., 2001: 355)

These authors use a different style from the outset: instead of using the personal pronoun, at this point, as in 'we investigate', for example, they choose a more impersonal style: 'The work . . . investigates'. The problem that this research addresses is defined earlier and more concisely than in the first example. Here the authors get much more quickly to the point of the research, providing less in the way of context and rationale for the work at this point in the abstract, though presumably there would be more of that in the paper itself.

The next sentence summarizes the results. The main line of argument is articulated, using the personal pronoun 'we' this time: developing an explanation, testing it, modifying it and testing it again. The process of iteration, in the research, is described concisely. A linking device is the use of 'we', at the start of three consecutive sentences, showing stages in the research: 'explain', 'test' and 'modify', although, interestingly, the last sentence does not begin with 'we', perhaps suggesting a more objective interpretation of the data?

A third example contains some similarities and displays further options for writers.

Journal abstract – example 3

Current views of the control of complex, purposeful movements **acknowledge that** organizational processes must reconcile multiple concerns. . . . Motor control **theorists have long recognized** the role of classical mechanics in theories of movement organization, **but** an appreciation of the importance of intrinsic interlimb bias has been gained **only recently.**

Although detailed descriptions of temporal coordination dynamics **have been provided, systematic attempts to identify** additional salient dimensions of interlimb constraint **have been lacking. We develop and implement** here a **novel** method for examining this problem by exploiting two robust principles of psychomotor behaviour, the symmetry constraint and the *Two-Thirds Power Law*. **Empirical evidence is provided** that the relative spatial patterns of concurrently moving limbs are naturally constrained in much the same manner as previously identified temporal constraints and, further, that apparent velocity interference is an indirect, secondary consequence of primary spatial assimilation. The **theoretical implications** of spatial interference **are elaborated** with respect to movement organization and motor learning. The need to carefully consider the appropriate dimensions with which to characterize coordination dynamics is also discussed.

(Walter et al., 2001: 393)

The starting point the authors chose for this abstract is a generalization about research in the field: this tells us what the subject of the research is and defines, in more than the one sentence quoted here, the underlying principles, indicated, presumably, by their use of the word 'must', suggesting that underpinning theory will not be challenged in this paper. There is then a distinction between this well-established theory and more recent thinking. As in the first two examples, the distinction between what is known and what remains to be researched is made quite clear: the difference is between 'detailed descriptions' and 'systematic attempts to identify'. In this abstract, the word 'lacking', like the words 'do not account for', 'none predict', 'problem' and 'failed' in the first two examples, identifies the need and focus for the research reported here. Similarly, a range of terms for 'branding' the contribution to research is used in these papers: 'accounts for', 'strengthens the interpretation of', 'explain', 'account for', 'empirical evidence is provided' and 'theoretical implications . . . are elaborated'. Equally important, in all of these abstracts, is the 'matching' of the type of problem identified, the type of research conducted and the type of conclusions drawn.

The personal pronoun, while not available in all disciplines, is clearly an option in this journal, although it is interesting to note, as in example 2, precisely where it is and is not used, that is, at which points in the argument.

Journal abstract – example 4

Fodor **has argued** that observation is theory neutral, since the perceptual systems are modular, that is, they are domain-specific, encapsulated, mandatory, fast, hard-wired in the organism, and have a fixed neural architecture. **Churchland attacks** the theoretical neutrality of observation on the grounds that (a) the abundant top-down pathways in the brain suggest the cognitive penetration of perception and (b) perceptual learning can change in the wiring of perceptual systems. **In this paper I introduce** a distinction between sensation, perception, and observation and **I argue** that although Churchland is right that observation involves top-down processes, there is also a substantial amount of information in perception which is theory-neutral. **I argue** that perceptual learning does not threaten the cognitive impenetrability of perception, and that the neuropsychological research does not provide evidence in favour of the top-down character of perception. Finally, **I discuss** *the possibility of* an off-line cognitive penetrability of perception.

(Raftopoulos, 2001: 423)

This paper begins not with an overview of generally agreed principles or underlying theory, but with a summary of the debate, with two researchers set against each other, and the term 'attacks' suggesting the strength of the difference between two approaches. This representation of the discipline – or the sub-discipline within which this work sits – may be about how the field is constructed, in terms of the researchers who use different approaches and reach different conclusions, or it may be the author's construction.

In other words, how you represent your discipline, in your writing, may be influenced both by 'how it is' and by 'how you see it'. There are, after all, different ways of representing a discipline, particularly if the purpose of doing so is to create a context for your own work. To some academics, this is a contentious view: for them, an academic discipline is what it is, neutral and fixed. There is one way of representing it. In other disciplines, there is a perception that there are numerous ways of representing previous work, and even the principles on which it was based: as a set of underlying principles, as a collection of 'current views' or 'zooming in' to the opposition between two different approaches, as in example 4 above. Unusually, for some disciplines, the contribution is signalled here by the repeated use of 'I': 'I introduce . . . I argue . . . I argue . . . I discuss'. These assertions are somewhat offset by the use of 'possibility' in the last sentence.

The fifth and last example from this journal is the most unusual of all, because it interrogates the journal and the discipline itself, although in some disciplines this is acceptable and even, in places, invited.

Journal abstract – example 5

The aim of Schunn, Crowley and Okada's (1998) study is to address **the question** of whether the current state of cognitive science, as represented by *Cognitive Science* and the Cognitive Science Society, "reflects the multidisciplinary ideals of its foundation." To **properly** interpret and respond to their results, we need to ask a **prior question**: What *is* cognitive science's multidisciplinary ideal? There are at least two conceptions – a "localist" conception, which seems to be implicit in Schunn, Crowley and Okada's discussion, and a "holist" conception. **I argue** that while both have been endorsed by some cognitive scientists, there are reasons for preferring the holist conception. **I then consider** what Schunn, Crowley and Okada's findings tell us about the state of cognitive science in light of a holist approach and **report on an analysis** of the journal's contents which looks at the domain, subdomain, and cognitive capacity investigated.

(Von Eckardt, 2001: 453)

The subject of this research is therefore 'the current state' of the discipline itself, and this paper opens with a comment on what other scholars have said about it. That this paper will go beyond that view is clear in the word 'properly'. While the work reported here consists of 'analysis', the outcome of that analysis is not specified at the end of this abstract, though presumably it would be defined in the paper itself.

For academics who have analysed this abstract, and others like it in other disciplines, this approach raises the question of what you need to include in your abstracts. Some academics find example 5 ineffective, since it does not specify the contribution and therefore does not encourage you to read the paper. This judgement is often repeated; it is a common criterion applied by academics – but how relevant is it? This is another of the many instances where academics bring their own criteria to their analyses of published work – understandably – rather than broadening their repertoire of writing styles. This is not to say that academic writers are unaware of writing options; it seems to us reasonable to interpret their reactions as the result of the absence of this type of analytical work in their writing careers.

This analysis does reveal aspects of writing that you may not be aware of at a conscious level. This is what academics report. Even though you recognize the quality of published papers in your discipline, you may be less clear about how precisely that quality is constructed. Many academics are not sure how to define the techniques they see in academic writing. One potential effect of this lack of knowledge is uncertainty about what constitutes excellence in writing, and this can undermine a writer's confidence. Another potential effect is insensitivity to the subtle distinctions mapped out by different techniques. That is why analysis of texts forms a major section of this chapter. Without this level of analysis, there is a risk that they will not make the adjustments to your writing so as to produce features that they know are currently acceptable in their discipline.

Another way of analysing published work, building on the above analyses, is to focus on one point in the argument and define the way in which that is handled in each abstract. For example, you can learn a lot about your target journal by lining up all the opening sentences, that point where the rationale of each paper is established, or problem to be addressed is articulated:

1 **Working memory resources are needed** for processing and maintenance of information during cognitive tasks. Many models have been developed to capture the effects of limited working memory resources on performance.

(Daily et al., 2001: 315)

2 **The work presented here investigates** the process by which one group of individuals solves the problem of detecting deceptions created by other agents.

(Johnson et al., 2001: 355)

3 **Current views of the control of** complex, purposeful movements acknowledge that organizational processes must reconcile multiple concerns. . . . Motor control theorists have long recognized the role of classical mechanics in theories of movement organization, but an appreciation of the importance of intrinsic interlimb bias has been gained only recently.

(Walter et al., 2001: 393)

4 **Fodor has argued that** observation is theory neutral, since the perceptual systems are modular, that is, they are domain-specific, encapsulated, mandatory, fast, hard-wired in the organism, and have a fixed neural architecture. Churchland attacks the theoretical neutrality of observation.

(Raftopoulos, 2001: 423)

5 **The aim of Schunn, Crowley and Okada's (1998) study is** to address the question of whether the current state of cognitive science, as represented by *Cognitive Science* and the Cognitive Science Society, 'reflects the multidisciplinary ideals of its foundation'

(Von Eckardt, 2001: 453)

Looking at these sentences separately from the paper allows you to focus on the details of the differences. Using a highlighter pen for this type of analysis is a simple but effective way of isolating specific features of academic writing across a range of texts.

You can, of course, do this type of analysis on other points in the paper – not just the abstract. You might, for example, find it instructive to analyse a completely different stage in the argument, such as how the research reported is recontextualized in the literature, towards the end of the paper.

As Reder and Schunn (1999 . . .) have noted, two distinct approaches to studying individual differences have been employed in the field. . . . **Our work is an example of this second approach with the additional feature that we used** a computational model to predict and explain the differences in working memory performance among individual subjects. **It is interesting to note the similarities and differences between our approach and that developed within** . . . **Though previous research has highlighted** that individual differences exist, these differences have not been modelled at the level of the individual subject. That **we were able to do so** speaks to the power of our approach . . .

(Daily et al., 2001: 349)

In many journals, in many disciplines, papers conclude with this type of direct comparison with other studies and an explicit statement of what the study has contributed to the field. Precisely which words you use to articulate this, where you put them in your paper, and how long and detailed you make this section depend not only on the nature of your work and your conclusions, but also on the journal you are writing for. These and other conventions may be in use in journals in your discipline at this time, and they may be very familiar to you, but it is usually worth investing some time in developing your knowledge of the journals further.

In addition, you can analyse how the contents of abstracts are developed in the paper itself:

1 How is the structure of the abstract mapped out in sections of the paper?
2 Are there verbal links – such as repeated key terms – between abstract and paper?
3 Is material provided in the paper that was not in the abstract?
4 Do the proportions of the abstract match those of the paper?

Analysing journals in these terms, across several papers and perhaps several recent issues, gives you a detailed knowledge and conscious awareness of academic writing in your discipline. You may not get this simply from reading in your discipline, and you may take longer to learn as much from reviewers' feedback. You can, of course, consult experienced, successful writers: what are their perceptions? How do they define the qualities of academic writing that are currently valued in your discipline? How do they go about producing those? Have they analysed published writing in your discipline in this – or any other – way and/or have they internalized, over time, the structures and styles required for published writing in your discipline?

The issue of the journal that was the subject of analysis in this chapter, *Cognitive Science*, not only looked across the field, including different approaches, but also, in this issue, interrogated itself – in abstract 5 – where there was discussion of interdisciplinarity and the role of interdisciplinary work and approaches in this field. This discussion is relevant to other disciplines: interdisciplinarity is on numerous agendas, as boundaries are broken down and disciplines work together. In this context, there is all the more reason for you to study and acknowledge the value of rhetorics and genres in other disciplines than your own. It may be, of course, that several genres are already available in your discipline – as represented in academic journals – and even within journals.

Analysing journals: what can it tell you about disciplinarity?

- How disciplinarity is constructed.
- What forms of disciplinarity are available.
- Rhetorical strategies you can use to represent disciplinarity in your work.
- Ways of interrogating disciplinarity.

How can you use the information about academic writing that you collect in your analyses? Some academics tell us they find this form of analysis works as a driver for their writing. You may find, for example, that certain rhetorical modes – or ways of structuring an academic argument or paper – prompt you to think about your own work in similar terms. Many features of the abstracts analysed in this chapter could be used in other disciplines than Cognitive Science.

Having made such a strong case for this type of analysis, we have to acknowledge that some academics think that it is overstated, in the sense that they see academic writing as variable, and our search for norms, forms and conventions in each journal as superficial and simplistic. On the other hand, many academics are quick to assert that each discipline is distinctive, and that academic writing must therefore be, in every case, discipline-specific. From this perspective they often reject what they see as 'generic' approaches that cross disciplinary boundaries. Some academics hold both views: maintaining that academic writing in their disciplines has specific characteristics, although these cannot be 'reduced' to a set of common elements by means of rhetorical analysis.

Some academics challenge the outcome of this analysis in one or more rhetorical questions:

- Are you saying that all these writers consciously chose to write in this way?
- Are you saying that reviewers and editors of this journal only accept papers that are written in this way?
- Do you mean that if I write in a different way, my paper will be rejected?
- Surely there are many different styles in each journal?
- How can you generalize?
- What is your evidence that there are patterns in the writing published in journals?

These are questions that some academics ask us, when we analyse published papers in this way, as they assess the implications for academic writing generally and their writing specifically. This usually prompts us to repeat that, firstly, we do not argue that all papers for a specific journal are identical style and, secondly, that our analysis – and yours – constitutes a body of evidence on which to build a definition of disciplinarity. It also provides a solid basis for a strategic approach to constructing disciplinarity in your writing.

If you do this type of analysis on your target journals, you will establish not only what is expected of you, but also how you can sharpen your writing to strengthen it in specific ways. This may take time. You will also be building your expertise through writing over the course of many submissions and, of course, resubmissions.

Your learning process may be a matter of gradually recognizing and incorporating features of scholarship in your thinking and writing. At first, the rhetoric of your discipline may seem constraining, but over time you may see it as liberating, as it helps you to sift through aspects of your research, to work out what is worth writing about and to be confident that you know how to go about it.

Developing your own 'voice'

Academic writers often say that they worry that they are losing their own voice, or wonder if they are ever going to develop one. They spend so long reading and analysing other people's writing that they feel they lose sight of what they want to say and how they want to write. This is such a recurring topic, and genuine concern, that it might be something you should address.

The desire to find a personal voice may stem from a fear of being overwhelmed by the authority of published writing. Is there a risk of your ideas being swamped by others', as you write? Or, given the level of detail we suggest for your analysis of journals, is there a possibility that you will feel that there is no room for your own 'rhetoric'? New writers in particular sometimes have an emotional response: that shaping their ideas in certain ways, so as to be able to join the published debate in journals, will compromise their values.

Is the issue of voice associated with finding your own position in the debate and articulating that distinctiveness in conceptual/intellectual, discipline-specific terms? This may be where academic writers begin to feel that they are losing their voice. If you have not published much or at all in your discipline, you may still be in the process of finding your place in the debate.

However, developing your own voice may not be an achievable goal in academic writing. For new writers particularly, there are other goals. Trying to develop your own voice may distract you from them. In addition, your authority in writing is always in question, seemingly always contingent on other people's evaluations, and writing in your own 'voice' will not change this.

Does the search for a voice originate in a fear of loss of identity in the discipline? While the question of 'voice' in writing may take us into a discussion of style, perhaps we could more usefully focus on 'voice' in the sense of 'contribution'? Perhaps writers who fear losing their voice could reconceptualize 'voice' as 'contribution'; academic writing in your discipline does, presumably, require you to articulate your view of the field and your own contribution to it. In a sense, this is your 'voice'.

Checklist

- Define the characteristics of writing in your discipline.
- Analyse recent issues of journals in your discipline.
- Focus on and compare specific points in several papers.
- Work out how you can adapt your writing for different journals.
- Decide how you want to position yourself in your discipline.
- Consider your options for 'voicing' this position in your writing.

Part II

It's all very well coming to terms with the characteristics and rhythms of academic writing. And for many, this is probably a necessary process. But unless you are naturally supported in your writing activities at work, writing can be a very difficult thing to find the time and the motivation to do. Part II describes and evaluates three specific interventions that we have conducted many times in academic settings. Each of them is designed to support and nourish writing habits in different ways, and each of them has a focus on helping participants to produce scholarly output. Chapters 5, 6 and 7 describe three supportive professional development interventions: writers' retreats, writing for publication programmes and writers' groups. If you are interested in initiating, participating in or developing these kinds of supports within your own institutional setting, these chapters will give you enough detail to get a good picture of what they involve and what is needed in order to run them effectively.

5

Retreating to advance

Planning, running and participating in writers' retreats for academics

Introduction • The context for academic writers' retreats • What is a writers' retreat? • Rationale for a writers' retreat • How to prepare for a writers' retreat • During the retreat • After the retreat • Positive expectations • Concerns • Outcomes • Writers' retreat and gender • Variations on the balance between collective writing space and private writing spaces • Variations on the five-day, residential model • Key moments and experiences facilitated by the retreat environment • Conclusions

Introduction

This chapter takes you through the aims, processes and options associated with writers' retreats for academics. It gives you all the information and advice you need to consider running a writers' retreat in your own context and provides a checklist for planning, delivering and following up on an effective retreat. Primarily, it shows how this particular strategy can be another significant pillar of support when it comes to developing and enhancing academic writing in a whole range of different settings. The retreat phase (explored in Chapter 3) is different from the retreat experience, which we outline in this chapter. The writers' retreat experience is a specific event in which people retreat from their normal world in order to make significant and focused advances in their writing.

The context for academic writers' retreats

In academia, as well as in other creative contexts, original ideas are often remote or far removed from the problem that they are designed to solve (see for example, Gruber, 1988 and Runco, 2004a). Sometimes academic writers need to get away from everything familiar and routine in order to make positive writing progress or to enhance their writing tasks. It is this basic principle of creativity that has encouraged some higher education institutions to initiate writers' retreats, a professional development innovation that is the focus of this chapter.

For many years, the notion of creating safe spaces for writing has been used by writers as a serious and legitimate route to writing development. Creative writers all over the world have benefited from time that is both separate and different from their normal life and working schedules. The existence of writing sanctuaries is a reflection of the fact that good writing is an important, special and focused activity that at least occasionally needs special spaces and times in which it isn't just a priority, but in which, for even a short time, it is the only focus of attention.

Academic writers often need to try to fit their writing times into relatively short slots around the other activities of their professional lives. In Chapter 1, we showed how effective writing rhythms can be created relatively simply by designing short writing slots. However, doing only this kind of writing may eventually serve to exacerbate the sense of fragmentation that academics often report when talking about their professional lives (Grant and Knowles, 2000). We have seen that it is extremely useful to make deliberate room for longer swathes of writing at key times in the academic year or at crucial stages in a specific writing project.

Of course, any academic can individually try to negotiate a situation in which they retreat from their working world and normal responsibilities for a block of time. The traditional university-based sabbatical system provides an example of institutional recognition of the need for time and space in which to pursue and develop ideas in writing. Some universities do have established policies that protect time for academics to write, but many do not. These days sabbaticals and other forms of protected writing time may be much more difficult to secure than they have been in the past. Besides, the extent to which they actually do help people to make dramatic progress in a writing task has been questioned (Boice, 1987) and at the very least, varies radically from person to person.

Nevertheless, if higher education institutions expect their faculty to do the kind of creative work that we argue is part of any writing task, it is necessary for them to recognize that people sometimes need special, dedicated, supported time (see, for example, Runco, 2004b).

By describing writers' retreats, this chapter presents a practical alternative to extended leave for academics, recognizing that such extended leave may be impossible for many, but also that academic writers can benefit hugely from dedicated blocks of time focusing solely on their writing (Grant and Knowles, 2000; Moore, 2003; Murray, 2004). Introducing writers' retreats to academic settings has sometimes been viewed as a very innovative and unusual step, taken by radical educational developers or extremely committed groups of academics who really want to develop and progress their writing while also helping one another. Instead of being seen as unusual or quirky interventions in some academic environments, we suggest that if well supported and managed, writers' retreats could become a commonplace and effective mechanism for improving writing processes, outputs and quality both on an individual and institutional basis. We think that such initiatives should not be seen as an unusual or left of centre activity for bleeding-heart educational developers, or as remedial interventions designed to support 'unproductive' or 'non-research-active' faculty. Rather, we would like to see writers' retreats become a normal part of many academic landscapes, recognizing and supporting as they do the significant pressures brought to bear on all academic writers, experienced or otherwise.

In addition, writers' retreats are a holistic mechanism, supporting academic writing in ways that celebrate, sustain and take care of writers in an intensive and compressed time frame. They invoke creative responses and routines that can kick-start or enhance an individual academic writing strategy. Their regular existence and support may also serve to valorize and endorse the institution's commitment to academic writing, reflecting the significant contributions that academic writing makes to academia, not only in terms of published output, but also in terms of the value associated with sharing insights, helping one another to achieve breakthroughs, building effective strategies and creating new and collective orientations towards topics and ideas.

Writers' retreats are often the first contexts within which many academics have discussed and shared their writing strategies and processes with others. Retreats may be one of the arenas within which academic writers can develop their work in an optimum environment. These kinds of temporary environments have the potential to benefit not just individual subjects or disciplines, but also academia as a whole.

Since writers' retreats were initiated at the University of Limerick in 2001, more than 150 academics have benefited from their existence, and the retreat intervention has been extended and used in Ireland by inter-university networks (see O'Neill, Moore and McMullin, 2005). Given the disproportionate numbers of women who choose to participate, they are initiatives that seem to be more appealing to women academics than their male counterparts. The reasons for this will be discussed later in this chapter.

What is a writers' retreat?

A writers' retreat is a developmental initiative that is:

- A pragmatic way of allocating a dedicated block of time to academic writing.
- An event that provides intensive, holistic, symbolic and practical support for all aspects of the writing process.
- An event that recognizes the physical, psychological, academic and collegiate needs of academic writers.
- An event characterized by hard work in the context of a healthy, stress-free, enjoyable week.
- An event that enhances output.
- An event that aims to give rise to more productive writing habits in the longer term.
- An event that encourages creative engagement in academic writing tasks.

Rationale for a writers' retreat

The rationale for a writers' week is based on previous evidence that people and the quality of their ideas can derive enormous benefits from a short-term intensive writing environment (Grant and Knowles, 2000). Writers' retreats have already been found to facilitate the achievement of an exclusive focus on writing by creating an arena in which the normal distractions of work and life are temporarily removed (Moore, 1995). This can serve to initiate, to nourish or to accelerate writing, even if standard writing habits need to be sustained in different ways during the normal course of professional daily life. Despite operating in educational environments, university faculty report that it is often difficult to achieve an exclusive focus on writing in a way that can be facilitated by a retreat environment (Cameron, 1999).

The logistics of collaboration, interaction and peer support often depend on private, informal networks that many people simply don't have access to. Through participation in writers' retreats, such support can be created more deliberately and with more beneficial effects.

The retreat environment creates a context within which a community of practice can be initiated and enhanced more quickly and easily, concrete outcomes can be achieved, and a precedent for collaborative dialogue (both written and spoken) can be set. This rationale echoes the objectives originally associated with the writers' retreats that have been running in New

Zealand, Australia, Ireland, the UK and in several universities in the USA, that is:

> to create an atmosphere of trust and safety for productive writing; to help participants to learn from each other about the process of writing; to create a multidisciplinary community of writers who would provide support and advice to one another both during the retreat and beyond; to explore the important links between teaching, research, writing and scholarship; and to have a productive working experience in which each participant would commit to a specific writing goal and try to achieve it [within the time frame of the retreat].
>
> (Moore, 2003: 335)

Writers' retreats have been designed, then, to operate as temporary writing 'sanctuaries' away from the normal rhythms of professional life. Some of the benefits that can be more easily created in a retreat context include the achievement of exclusive focus on writing, total immersion in the writing process, the creation of a nurturing environment which gives people the courage to face their struggles and uncertainties with the writing process, and the creation of norms in which people who typically do not share their work become more accustomed and inclined to do so.

Because it is still an unusual and unconventional way of working and collaborating, it often feels like a daring and somewhat complicated experiment, and one that requires much planning and preparation both on a personal and a professional level. Despite these complexities, the format tends to contain relatively simple elements.

With the right support, writers' retreats can be organized independently by interested groups of academics, or through help from centres of educational development or institutional units designed to promote or resource academic practice. Given that writers' retreats require financial support and still represent a rather novel way of helping academics to develop their writing, it is very useful to have a champion at a senior level within your university. However, given how useful they can be for individual academics, this senior-level support should not be considered necessary to ensure that the retreat model is implemented successfully.

We have organized retreats that have been supported and funded by senior university management, as well as those that have been run on an independent, inter-university, voluntary basis. Both models have produced the same kinds of positive results, though the latter does require more commitment from participants in terms of planning, funding and organization.

How to prepare for a writers' retreat

Good writers' retreats need good locations. A writers' retreat should be what it says it is: a complete get-away from the normal academic environment, far enough away from the usual campus location that participants are not tempted to nip back intermittently as work commitments lure them away from the reasons they needed to retreat in the first place. Because a retreat is residential, the location needs to offer comfortable accommodation in which every participant ideally can set up his or her own private writing space. A hotel or a conglomeration of self-catering houses can work well. We have sometimes used large B&Bs, as long as there are enough rooms to accommodate everyone. There are practical requirements that residential accommodation should satisfy in order to provide the ideal environment for a writers' retreat.

Checklist for writers' retreat accommodation

1 Peace and quiet.
2 Separate, private writing areas.
3 Good-sized desks and desk lamps for all participants.
4 A common seminar area for writing workshops and facilitated sessions.
5 Plenty of plugs and or extension leads in this common area to facilitate communal writing sessions using laptops.
6 Facilities that can be used exclusively by participants to print work in progress.
7 Well-organized but flexible meal times that take into account the writing rhythms of participants.

Equipment

In preparation for a writers' retreat, organizers should bring the following communal equipment: plenty of A4 printing paper, staples and staplers, a printer and spare laptop (if this is not supplied on location), flip charts, pens, notebooks and coloured markers for creative sessions and ideas, and a 'library' of helpful references, readings and books (for many good suggestions, see the Bibliography at the end of this book).

Pre-retreat preparation

As well as making decisions about a location and being aware of equipment requirements, identifying a critical mass of participants is of course another crucial step. This can be as informal a process as asking colleagues if they would be interested in joining a collective of academic writers for a few days of intensive writing, or it can involve advertising the event through internal mail or networks. We have run writers' retreats with groups as small as 10 and as large as 26. At some retreats, participants have all been from the same academic department, while at other times, academically diverse individuals have formed a retreat group. The mix of people does tend to affect the dynamics of the group. A whole group of completely new writers can form a retreat, but we have found that it is a good idea to have at least some seasoned writers within the retreat who can share their struggles and triumphs with the rest of the group.

Identifying key facilitators

Ideally, every writers' retreat should have at least one key facilitator. While not absolutely necessary, it is worth finding someone outside of your academic context to play this role. You should try to recruit someone who is a credible academic writer, who understands the academic environment, who is supportive and facilitative, and who is sensitive to the fears and anxieties that are often invoked when academics decide to tackle particular academic writing projects, particularly in such a non-traditional, collaborative context. The facilitator should plan to run short writing workshops on different aspects of the writing process (see suggested programme later in this chapter) as well as to read and comment on pieces of writing that participants produce. However, if it is difficult to find a single facilitator, another option is to co-opt participants themselves to lead short workshops on different themes, skills, experiences or projects that relate to their academic writing. Both these formats have worked well in retreats that we have been involved in.

Briefing and preparing participants

Writing in a retreat environment is, as we have noted, still a novel way of engaging in any writing task. This makes it all the more important that participants prepare and orientate themselves in advance. They can assist one another in doing this by setting specific goals, deciding on target journals, and making a commitment to pursuing a particular writing outcome. An appropriate goal for a five-day retreat might be the production of a single written article. But the goals may vary from person to person. Some people can achieve significantly more, working on a number of connected projects, while others may need to set out more modest goals. Having a good writing facilitator run a preparatory session about two months in advance of the retreat can help people to set goals that are appropriate to their own stage of development.

Once you have recruited the retreat participants, you need to make sure that everyone prepares well in advance of the event in order to make the most of the intensive dedicated writing time that a retreat provides. This may involve quite intensive preparatory work including data-gathering, research, reading and collecting key literature and references.

Checklists for participants

Each participant needs to have a full information pack explaining briefly the purpose and goals of the retreat, suggesting key activities that need to be completed before embarking on the retreat, providing practical information about the location, travel arrangements and facilities at the retreat location.

Summary handouts for all participants might look like the following.

Handout 1: Getting ready: preparing for writers' retreat

- Read pre-retreat information pack carefully.
- Start organizing your materials NOW – data, references, important articles, any preparatory writing you have done.
- Start outlining the work you're planning to do.
- Make key decisions about your work well in advance of the week: for example target journal/publisher/format/genre.

Handout 2: Targeting a journal (adapted from Murray, 2004)

Experts in effective academic writing strategies say: 'Do not write and then plan to find an appropriate "place" for your writing – rather, analyse target journals carefully and then write with the benefit of this analysis.'

- Get several copies and scan recent editions of your chosen journal.
- Read full instructions for authors, check website and print off all relevant author information.
- Work out how you can mould your work to suit the journal's agenda.
- Write to the editor with an initial inquiry.

Emailing the editor
'I am writing a paper on XXX which argues that YYY. . . Do you think this would be of interest to readers of the journal at this time?'

If you get a response, reply thanking the editor and letting him/her know when the paper is likely to be completed.
This relatively easy exercise does several things:

- It externalizes your commitment to writing.
- It means that you won't be 'writing into the dark', but that you'll have a specific goal in advance of the writers' retreat.
- It has the pragmatic effect of differentiating your paper from those that are submitted without an 'initial go-ahead' from the editor.

Handout 3: Before the retreat

- Prepare to transport your laptop or arrange to borrow one.
- Prepare a short outline of your writing project and email it to all other participants. If you wish, include a copy of your email inquiry to a journal editor, and any responses you have received.
- Commit to keeping a record of the 'ecology' of your paper (versions, correspondence, feedback, reviews, ideas, changes in direction and so on). This will become a helpful professional development tool for yourself and your colleagues.
- Make your transport arrangements well in advance. Decide if you are going to drive.
- Commit to the ENTIRE week. It is far away. It is residential. You need to ensure that you are not so stressed on arrival that it takes 24 hours before you are in the right frame of mind to start writing.

Some reading:

- A paper on the writers' retreat concept (Moore, 2003).
- A chapter from Rowena Murray's book: *Writing for Academic Journals*, Chapter 2: 'Targeting a journal'.

These handouts should be distributed at a pre-retreat meeting, if possible. If a real-time meeting is impossible, then they are even more useful in providing good frameworks for everyone to help them prepare and focus on what they want to achieve before, during and after the retreat.

During the retreat

So, participants gather in an off-campus location equipped with ideas, data and literature they have gathered in order to be prepared to complete a piece of academic writing. Each of the five days is devoted to individual writing time, punctuated with opportunities for feedback from colleagues, group or paired meetings to discuss progress, and opportunities to exchange shared writing experiences. Every day begins with a facilitated session that provides structured advice on writing. Participants gather in the evenings for social interaction and dinner in a central location, and for further discussion on the writing projects in which each of them is engaged.

Sample schedule for a five-day writers' retreat

Sunday evening	Participants arrive, set up their writing spaces and attend a short workshop led by the facilitator on the aims and values of writers' retreats.
Monday:	Springboard session 1: Setting goals for your academic writing. Two hours of communal writing and idea exchange; individual writing time. Afternoon: session on ideas for sharing work in progress; writing time.
Tuesday:	Springboard session 2: Targeting journals and crafting your writing. Afternoon: session setting up writing partnerships and sharing work in progress.
Wednesday:	Springboard session 3: Dealing with bad reviews and negative criticism. Communal writing session focusing on reviewing and enhancing first drafts. Private writing time.
Thursday:	Springboard session 4: Developing a longer-term writing strategy. Starting to address a longer-term strategy and reflect on the ways in which writing in a retreat context can be installed into daily, and weekly, writing habits in normal work environments.
Friday:	Springboard session 5: Maintaining momentum and motivation in academic writing. Finish.

After the retreat

Evaluating the impact of the retreat

Organizing, designing and delivering writers' retreats costs money, time and significant energy. Retreats usually benefit from support of senior management, and must be 'worth it' from both an institutional and individual perspective. Real results must accrue from the intervention in ways that can be demonstrated through increased quantity and quality of publication in academic journals. However, the more qualitative transformations that individuals experience are also valuable to capture and report. People don't usually become successful academic writers overnight. Any writers' retreat intervention should also examine the insights and reflections of participants as well as providing additional support and networking when participants have returned to their normal work environments. Views, insights and outputs can be captured using pre- and post-writers' week questionnaires, which contain qualitative insights about the value and the impact of the experience.

However, when evaluating the impact of the retreat experience, it is important to emphasize that one of the central reasons why some academics find it difficult to write stems from the sense of institutional surveillance they feel is applied to their academic writing. If there is an over-emphasis on monitoring the short-term written outputs associated with the writers' retreat, this may undermine one of the very reasons that academics give for wanting to participate. The pressure to produce written output already exists within most universities. We believe that retreats can be professional development experiences that help academic writers to respond more effectively to that pressure, rather than being a mechanism for creating more of it.

Positive expectations

While existing research on the writers' retreat format shows that participants tend to express the need to 'get started', to 'hit the ground running' and to initiate a writing project (Grant and Knowles, 2000; Moore, 2003), the motives of the participants can vary. Several participants at different types of retreat have expressed a need to focus more on completing, on finishing and on pulling together many ideas in the form of a series of written pieces. The difference in individual retreat motives and goals can be attributed to differences in the stages of writing that each participant has already reached and also (at least in part) to differences in the pre-work and preparation in which members have been able or willing to participate in the months leading up to the writers' retreat.

Volunteer participant groups are by definition self-selecting and may be different from academics in general in so far as they may have a particularly strong need for space and time in which to contain and articulate their research and to develop their voices as academic writers. When asked to highlight the predicted benefits of writers' retreats, the most frequent responses highlight the importance of creating space and time in which to write, a function of the week to which participants generally seem to attribute the most value. In articulating their expectations, participants tend to talk about the importance of sharing wisdom, of getting feedback from their peers, of forging new links, of enhancing 'serious writing', and of the opportunities for creativity, collegiality, collaboration and enhanced commitment. In terms of more tangible outcomes, they tend to highlight the importance of producing effective and publishable written outputs in ways that will be useful for building their CVs and for ensuring their own professional development.

Concerns

Like almost any new endeavour, participants do not come to a retreat environment without at least some anxieties and concerns. They wonder if they will be able to write effectively without the framework of information access that they could avail of in their normal settings, they express concerns about building and maintaining writing-related momentum, they worry that they might get side-tracked by distractions, be unable to coordinate and integrate their writing, and that even given the extremely supportive and productive environment, they will still struggle to write, or more particularly struggle to write well. It is normal that these kinds of concerns are discussed during the course of the week, but also important that writing breakthroughs, successes and struggles continue to be understood and discussed once the retreat is over.

Outcomes

In addition to tangible outputs that usually come in the form of a completed paper/chapter/proposal, it is also worth noting the behavioural and attitudinal changes that participants report in their approach both to academic writing and to educational development. Participants tend to report having developed new strategies for producing important written work within their fields. They tend to highlight that the retreat experience helped them to refine, to structure, to express and to display ideas in a way that they found satisfying and personally empowering. Generally, a sense of group cohesiveness among participants is often mentioned as being an important 'by-product' of the retreat, as is the likelihood of interacting more frequently with others about their writing. These outcomes, if supported effectively on a longer-term basis, are likely to form the foundations for healthy, pleasurable and productive institutional writing patterns.

Writers' retreat and gender

From the time that we have been involved in academic writing development, we have always been struck by gendered aspects associated with interventions designed to help academic writers. This is particularly true of writers' retreats, in which female participants have always been in the large majority. At the

University of Limerick writers' retreats, out of an average group of 18 participants per retreat, it is unusual to have more than two or three male participants. In many cases, the retreats have been all female, despite the fact that the
event is advertised to all faculty regardless of gender or any other characteriztic. Bloom (1985) has argued that while male academics are just as likely to
struggle with their academic writing as their female counterparts, they seem
less likely to 'come forward', perhaps feeling that doing so represents an
admission of weakness or inadequacy. Others have argued that women academics may find it more difficult to justify time and space for writing either in
their professional or personal lives, and that the retreat is a new route for
helping them to do what they have found difficult to do in the course of the
normal rhythm and schedule of their lives (Nelson, 1993). It may be that men
and women either experience or attribute difficulties with writing differently
from one another, as suggested for example by Cayton, (1990) and therefore
pursue (or don't pursue) different kinds of solutions.

Availing of writers' retreats (or retreating to advance) seems to be a strategy
that is much more likely to appear in a woman's repertoire of writing development options than in that of men. Whatever the differences between
male and female academic writers, we have found two things to be true of the
retreat. Firstly, that women are more likely to sign up and participate, but
secondly, that the participating men report just as many benefits and positive
outcomes as do their female counterparts. It may be that this self-selecting
minority group has exceptional characteristics that are not shared by other
men. But we suspect that once men are convinced that writers' retreats are
relevant to them and their needs, they can derive the same benefits and
satisfaction from their participation as their female colleagues.

Variations on the balance between collective writing space and private writing spaces

We have experimented with different modes of writing in retreat contexts.
One of the decisions that it is useful to make when planning the retreat
schedule relates to how much time should be devoted to writing in private
solitary spaces, and how much to writing together in the same space. There are
advantages to both. Solitary writing space provides people with the privacy
they sometimes need to get going or to make progress and to pace their writing
and take their breaks according to their own rhythms. Working in a common
space, though, can contribute to what one participant referred to as a 'great
sense of togetherness', or a commonality of purpose, and, possibly for those
reasons, seems to give rise to the individual production of more text than
people produce when writing in their own spaces. This is not to say that

academic writing in this environment becomes a mechanistic production line or typing pool – but, particularly for writers who find it hard to stay motivated when writing alone, this context can give rise to higher levels of fluency and confidence.

Variations on the five-day, residential model

Perhaps blocking out five days for a retreat such as the one we have described above seems like an impossible task. It takes planning, organization and time. If you feel that it seems too much, but you would still like to benefit from the features of a retreat-like environment, you might also consider some of the following, less time-consuming retreat templates:

A one- or two-day, non-residential retreat

There are many academics who find it very difficult to commit to a five-day residential programme, no matter how much they would like to. Caring responsibilities, heavy work schedules and other factors may make such a commitment prohibitive. Alternatives to the residential model include a one- or two-day non-residential retreat where an intensive, exclusive focus on writing occurs during 'normal' working hours on a 9am to 5pm basis. Shorter facilitated springboard sessions like those outlined could punctuate writing activity and feedback on work in progress. While these types of retreat experience don't seem to facilitate the same level of immersion that residential retreat participants report, they do have many of the same benefits. In particular, participants do achieve constructive focus even within the somewhat more bounded time frames that they require.

Several punctuated retreat days over the course of two or three months

Another non-residential approach to writers' retreat involves scheduling four or five full days for retreating, over the period of several months. This can be particularly useful for adopting an 'evolutionary' approach to writing development, during which participants can trace the progress of their work and be helped to do this in an organized way with the assistance of dedicated facilitators. Careful planning, monitoring and tracking of participants' progress will help to ensure that each successive day will give rise to momentum and progress.

A weekend residential retreat

This is a more condensed form of the five-day residential model, and again facilitated sessions need to be carefully balanced with time for writing.

Specific-purpose retreats

Participants report that immersion, total focus, lack of distraction and the capacity to 'be present' in their writing are all benefits of the writers' retreat model. It is also possible that such benefits might be enhanced in certain ways when 'specific-purpose' retreats are organized in order to focus on particular types of academic writing. We have designed and delivered retreats that are departmentally based, with participants all coming from the same academic department and writing broadly within the same discipline. This seems to enhance subject-specific discussions, and while there may be a risk that such retreat groups might suffer from a lack of interdisciplinarity and self-conscious competition between participants, this has not been our experience.

Other retreats might also be organized specifically for:

- collaborative writing projects (when interaction may be even more important than when people are authoring their text alone);
- those who have been invited to revise and resubmit journal articles (when the issues of responding to challenging feedback might require particular focus and understanding);
- those converting their PhD research into a publishable output (when crafting, condensing and targeting writing may be of prime concern);
- those preparing research proposals (when proposal conventions and requirements should receive primary attention).

Key moments and experiences facilitated by the retreat environment

For us, the writers' retreat has always been an enormously satisfying and positive professional event. That participants generally feel the same is corroborated by the feedback they provide. Those who have run writers' retreats in other contexts seem to have similar insights (for example Grant and Knowles, 2000; Schneider, 2003; O'Neill, Moore and McMullin, 2005). Some of the key, recurring 'moments' or experiences that have come to characterize writers' retreats for us include the following: experimentation with different approaches to writing, stripping away of commonly used excuses for not writing, the development of a clearer understanding of the physiological rhythms that facilitate or prohibit writing, aligning know-how with actual practice and celebration of writing.

Because people give themselves the opportunity to become completely immersed in writing, they have more of a chance in the writers' retreat than they usually do to experiment with different time slots, different forms and different writing rhythms. They can carve up their writing days in ways that are normally impossible, thus gaining insights about the times of the day (and indeed night) that they feel at their best for writing. They can try out what it feels like to write in the same space as others, and balance this with writing in more secluded settings in order to see what seems to work best for them. All of these experiments are easier in a place where several days of uninterrupted time for writing have been allocated. For the same reasons, it becomes possible for people to confront some barriers to writing that may not, in other settings, be so obvious to them.

Given that many academics cite a lack of time when explaining to themselves and others why they have not made progress with their writing, the time issue becomes a focus of considerable reflection. At writers' retreats, large blocks of time stretch out in front of participants, an experience that is unusual for many of them. The removal of the time problem makes it possible to see other barriers more clearly, those that may have more to do with confidence, professional esteem, entitlement and a sense of competence. But it also gives them the time and space in which to invent and develop effective writing supports through the establishment of new routines, insights, peer partnerships and the like.

That writers' retreat is an event in which people actually write (not just talk about it or think about it or prepare to do it) is something that differentiates it from many other forms of writing development interventions. Proven techniques proposed by facilitators can be tested and applied almost immediately in the context of participants' current writing tasks. This alignment of know-how and practice is a significant characteriztic of the retreat environment.

But probably the most endorsing aspect of writers' retreat is what people say and do when they reach the end of this intensive writing experience. The final night of a retreat is often characterized by a sense of real delight and celebration, revealed in participants' spontaneous articulation of achievements that they had not predicted, breakthroughs that they had not expected, and insights about writing that might have been difficult to gain without this kind of immersion in their task.

Conclusions

Writers' retreats are designed to create time and space for writing in ways that are separate from and different to people's normal academic environments.

This chapter has explored some of the essential considerations that should be taken into account when planning, preparing for and implementing a retreat, either within or between institutions. We have found that both intra- and inter-university retreats work well, as do retreats set up for more specific academic writing purposes.

Characteristics of effective academic writers' retreats can be summarized as follows:

- An intensive writing sanctuary providing advice and support for participants' writing projects.
- Task-orientated, with each participant identifying and aiming to achieve definite writing goals and outputs.
- Time committed to exploring writing processes as well as writing outputs.
- A supported intervention that removes concerns about surveillance and destructive criticism about academic writing that people may have encountered elsewhere in their professional lives.
- A dedicated, significant period of time of between one and five days' duration, that balances facilitated, structured guidance and independent private time for writing.

6

A writing for publication programme

The challenge of writing for academic journals • Rationale • Stages • Structure • Writing 'buddies' • Monitoring meetings • A writing mentor • Evaluations • Checklist

The challenge of writing for academic journals

Many academics report that one of their most difficult writing tasks is writing the first paper for publication. However, even those who have published in journals say they still find the process very challenging and more time-consuming than they feel it should be. This may be because both new and relatively experienced writers are still developing a process for writing for academic journals and still looking for a 'formula'.

Academics with little or no experience of writing for publication regularly report that while they have both experience and evidence of success in other forms of academic writing, most having completed a doctorate, for example, when they come to write their first journal article they face a range of problems for which they consider they are not sufficiently prepared. Even those who have published can still be struggling to make the process 'manageable'. As one new writer put it, writing the first papers does not necessarily occur as a straightforward progression from previous academic writing:

> At the very early stages of the writing process, the step between an idea for a paper and actual publication is enormous. However, as the topic and themes are developed, target dates are set and initial drafts are subjected to

peer review, the enormous step is transformed into a series of more gradual steps interspersed with landings or stages for review and reflection. The whole process becomes more manageable.

Some of these problems may originate in lack of confidence, or simply in the difference between this writing task and others, but they may indicate a need for information about what writing for publication entails. What the writer quoted above described as a transformation from 'idea' to 'paper' and from 'enormous' to 'manageable', can be actively managed by writers through a writing for publication (WfP) programme: it creates a 'series of . . . steps' for writing an academic paper, and thereby enables participants to define their own steps, establish their own pace and adapt them for different writing projects.

The WfP programme described in this chapter is one way of enabling new and developing writers to consider writing for publication as a 'process' and to develop writing projects as they do so. In addition, if the programme runs for an extended period of time, such as 6 or 12 months, it gives participants time to refine their processes through both interaction with other writers and reflection on their own emerging processes. Moreover, as a review of literature on academic writing development shows, this mode is more effective than short-term interventions:

> We recommend that universities support the development of structured interventions for their staff in order to increase their writing for publication. A regular, ongoing arrangement seems to be most beneficial, with a format that can be adapted to meet the needs of attendees.
>
> (McGrail et al., 2006: 34)

This chapter and the next describe examples of 'structured interventions'. Our experience suggests that developing writers can benefit from structured and sustained support. In addition, directing resources – that is, time – to writing sends a positive signal to writers. A strength of this type of programme is that it gives writers time to adapt in various dimensions of writing: beliefs, behaviours, skills and approaches. The 'structured interventions' that underpin the approaches we propose are useful in facilitating the process of writing for publication.

This chapter describes the programme and other support strategies that may run alongside it, and proposes a monitoring framework for developing writers. Observations on the development processes that may be involved are included throughout. Participants' comments in evaluations and follow-up interviews are used to underscore key changes and benefits.

Rationale

While in some contexts the WfP programme might seem a radical approach, it has a history, having been run in numerous universities across the UK and in other countries. It has also been adapted for other institutions, such as health-care settings.

The programme was created in response to the stated needs of developing writers aiming to write papers for submission to journals. The aim was to develop a programme that would be developmental, rather than remedial, avoiding the stigma associated at that time with writing instruction. Building on materials developed for short courses and workshops, the WfP programme took a longer view, offering support throughout a writing project, supporting writers as they adapted their writing practices.

Initial responses to this mode included incredulity: surely academics would never own up to needing help with their writing? Yet there were some academics who recognized their need for support and were prepared to participate in a formal programme that would help them achieve their writing goals.

The target audience were those who considered themselves to be either new to this form of academic writing or still learning about it, and the purpose was to raise the standard of their writing, specifically for publication. The emphasis was on helping these writers to start, progress, complete and submit a paper during the programme. This was not, therefore, a case of separating theory from practice. From the outset, each participant was encouraged to identify a specific project in order to focus any learning and writing that occurred during the programme.

The WfP programme evolved and changed over the past ten years, to the point where we can say that it seems to work best when certain components are in place.

Defined stages in the writing process

Generally, writers seem to find it useful to experience this writing task as a process, with defined stages. Even if writers adapt this structure after the programme, it seems that the existence of a definite series of steps, whatever form this series may take, is very useful. It seems to help writers to make progress in developing a piece of writing for publication. Participants' responses to the approach are the focus of regular discussions. These discussions have, over the years, provided insights into academic writing practices, adding to our understanding and that of participating writers.

The literature on academic writing

That there is such a literature comes as a surprise to many academics. Generally, academics do not learn about academic writing by reading about it. Once they are aware of the range of material in this field, they not only adopt established strategies, but many also adapt them for their teaching in order to help students with their writing. The WfP programme introduces writers to a range of strategies, some of which will be familiar, others not. The programme includes writing activities from the outset, so that participants try out new strategies for themselves. This combination of scholarly and practical approaches is probably important for academics in particular, but it adds credibility and is persuasive for other audiences.

'Tuning' writing skills

Taking a scholarly approach to writing helps academics 'tune' their understanding both of the components of good writing and of the process of producing it. Sustaining the programme over six months means that there is time for participants to individualize and contextualize new knowledge.

Journal requirements

While academics are likely to be familiar with journals in their field, as readers, they may not have absorbed the journals' requirements of writers. The WfP programme allocates time for analysis of journals that participants are targeting. The programme includes more detailed analysis of journal articles than academics generally perform.

The aims of a WfP programme should clearly be shaped by participating writers, and the framework described in this chapter can be adapted to different groups, but the core elements have worked well for dozens of groups of academics (and for others engaged in writing for publication at other institutions).

The programme helps writers to adopt a relatively linear strategy for a writing project, while building in a tolerance for iteration and reiteration, along with a structure for progressing through these stages, which often seem problematic and even disruptive to developing writers. Working in this way, they can experience what we have termed the 'advance-retreat' mode of academic writing: the linear structure characterizes writing as persisting in 'advance' mode, while the range of writing strategies employed at each meeting allows participants to continue to write even when they feel that their writing is in 'retreat' mode. This advance-retreat dynamic may be unavoidable, which is why we use the term 'tolerance for iteration'. Although the programme is linear, it is unlikely that participants will progress in a linear way in their writing; instead, the programme helps them to develop dynamic strategies.

The Wf P programme may not work for everyone. There have been drop-outs in each programme, and those who completed the programme did not find that it solved all their problems. Some writers did not submit a completed piece of writing within the time frame set out in the programme. In some instances, the programme merely highlighted a need for further resources, and for some writers it served as a test either of their commitment to writing or of the feasibility of their proposed writing projects. However, for many writers, the programme had a lasting positive effect on their writing, raising their awareness, facilitating a more deliberate, structured approach, and helping them to enhance their chances of publication.

Stages

The original aim of this programme for developing writers was to bring struc-ture to the writing process. We considered the literature on academic writing. In addition, we discussed writing with writers in various disciplines and noted that many of them had developed their own writing processes. We also asked intending participants – who did not at that point know what form the writing programme would take – what they expected to gain from a writing for publi-cation programme. Here are one group's responses, with specific expectations in bold.

What do developing academic writers need?

- Improved **writing skills** . . . Improved **management skills**.
- To learn more about the **writing process**, gain **insight into different writ-ing styles** with a view to perhaps changing or adapting my own method, which is perhaps not working to its full potential.
- To learn, develop and integrate **strategies for increasing the output** of my thinking and writing. To **enjoy writing** more than before. To **write regularly** for sustained projects.
- Well-defined **structure** . . . more **discipline** and the **ability to talk** through 'stuff' with others.
- I want to acquire **skill** in writing. **Confidence** in writing.
- The **habit** of writing regularly. . . . The **ability** to form journal articles and conference articles with greater **facility**. **Confidence** in my own ability as an academic writer.
- Published papers! In a nutshell. A more **sophisticated approach** to the formulation and execution of writing, more **focused** on specific journals.
- To develop a **practice** of academic writing that is regular and integral to my job as an academic. To develop a **collegiate approach** with colleagues to sustain that writing for me and for them in the future.

- To develop a writing **style** that meets needs for academic **rigour** but retains a 'readable' quality. To clarify **objectives in my professional career** and understand how research writing will assist. To succeed in the sense of learning process and technique rather than succeed in the sense of getting articles published.

These responses show that in one group there was a wide range of interests and stated needs, and this range occurred in a large number of groups. One feature that recurred in many such lists is writers' dual focus on output and process: they wanted to 'publish papers' but also 'learn more'. They also include the desire for behavioural change – more 'discipline', for example – and social effects – a 'collegiate approach'. The affective and emotional dimensions of writing are also present in 'enjoy' and 'confidence'. In other words, just about every component of writing appears on this one group's list, and some of the writers included more than one component in their brief statements. The implications for the design of a W*f*P programme were that it would be a mistake to focus on any one of these to the exclusion of the others.

Before each programme, we also ask intending participants what their writing goals are. The following responses from the same group show a predominant, but not exclusive, focus on writing journal articles and different interpretations of the word 'goal':

What are developing academic writers' goals?

- To produce a competitive or working **conference** paper with a view to presentation for **journal** publication.
- My writing goals are two-fold, or rather one goal is a consequence of the other. My first goal is to write and complete the **PhD thesis**. The second consequential goal is to write for publication, **journals and conferences**.
- To rework my Masters dissertation for publication as a **research note** in the [journal title].
- My goal perhaps would be that of actual achievement – a bottom line, the end of the road – literature review, review **article**, whatever, but something at least more tangible than just a *goal*.
- In the short term I would aim to produce one **paper** for [journal title] focusing on a literature review relevant to my thesis research.
- A journal **article** by [month] for [journal title] on [topic].
- I am currently finishing one **paper**, and look forward to at least finishing another one before starting the next one.
- My writing goal is to complete an **article** that is fit for publication and can be presented at a conference.
- To produce **paper** to work with. To learn discipline. To develop my own style. To increase confidence.

In this list there appeared to be more agreement in the group: there was a clear, common focus on output. The implications were that every participant should progress the specified project in the course of the WfP programme. In addition, given this focus on outputs, it was likely to be important to develop and discuss a range of dynamics at different stages in the programme, not just at the end. This suggested that participants should be encouraged to define their own outputs for each meeting.

Taking all this formal and informal, published and unpublished material into account, we designed a programme that established three stages in the academic writing process. Participants' evaluations, in numerous programmes, indicated that focusing on a specific goal was important in helping them move beyond intention to write to completing a paper: 'Having identified a publication at the outset as a target, this remains in focus, rather than being just a vague aspiration with an unspecified deadline.'

A six-month writing for publication programme

Stage 1: Months 1 and 2

1 Defining the writing goal.
2 Drafting the abstract.
3 Outlining the paper.

Stage 2: Months 3 and 4

4 Outlining the paper in detail: headings and sub-headings.
5 Writing regularly.
6 Giving and receiving peer review.

Stage 3: Months 5 and 6

7 Drafting the introduction and review of literature (with feedback).
8 Writing full draft (with feedback).
9 Revising drafts of all sections (with feedback).
10 Dealing with and responding to feedback from journals and resubmitting.

Mapping out stages and tasks in this way seemed like a modest adjustment to some writers, but a major imposition for others. For example, while 'Draft abstract' appears as step 2 in the programme, some writers were adamant that they could not write the abstract until they had written the paper. This is not to say that there is only one point at which the abstract should be drafted; instead, the activity of writing an abstract, and our differing understandings of its position in the academic writing process, challenged some writers' assumptions and, in time, changed some writers' long-standing habits.

Whatever the structure imposed on the writing process, and whatever the stages defined for that process, the key strength of the WfP programme is that it is mapped over real time. For each programme 'Months 1 and 2' would list two specific months. Time slots would be allocated for each meeting, in advance, for the whole six months, thus stimulating writers to think about their writing in terms of specific time slots.

The WfP programme was founded on the assumption that participants have something worth writing about. Precisely what their topics will be is the focus of several important discussions of writers' ideas and their target journals. Writers identify the gaps and links they can create between their ideas and the content of published articles. These gaps will be wide for some writers but narrow for others, and making connections between their work and other work reported in journals will be straightforward for some writers but complicated for others.

This is part of the work of a writing programme: to help participants, at the start, to establish where they might fit in the world of published academic debate and, if they consider that there is no place for them there, what they might do to find a place elsewhere. This may mean starting a higher degree or writing a research proposal, rather than a journal article, and these are important outputs for individuals and institutions alike.

This brings participants to an important discussion of the purpose of academic writing: what are their personal and professional aims? Each participant will have a particular view on this, and it is probably important that there is time to discuss each writer's individual balance of the professional and the personal. For some developing writers, this is a time to vent frustration with external assessments, for example. Without this discussion, there is a risk that such frustration could lead to disenchantment or cynicism about academic publishing.

One outcome of this discussion may be a broadening of writers' interpretations and uses of the term 'research'. For example, it is possible for participants to develop writing about 'applied' research (Furlong and Oancea, 2005), or to write about developments in practice or to write about their experience. For some, the key is simply to find an outlet for the kind of writing they can do. This programme can be used to prompt writers to make connections between what they want to 'say' in their writing and what they see in the journals.

While experienced writers would find this discussion relatively straightforward, developing writers, including new researchers, postgraduates and those working in disciplines where research is a new activity, have found this discussion demystifying, focusing and confidence-building. For many academics, discussing these issues in a group brought the added interest of hearing about other people's plans, revealed potential links between projects, and sometimes helped writers to experiment with new approaches to writing. It frequently left them more ready to adapt their existing strategies.

There is also added value in discussion for academics who say that they normally have very little time to talk about their research, although when they do, they enjoy it, find it useful and are stimulated by new synergies.

However, discussion is only part of the work of any meeting in the programme. There must also be time for writing, even as participants are defining their topics. This is where academics in a range of disciplines begin to see the value of freewriting (Elbow, 1973) and generative writing (Boice, 1990) in helping them to write in exploratory, even uncertain, ways, so as to make a start. The W*f*P programme can be an appropriate context in which to apply the principles of 'advance' and 'retreat' that we have outlined in chapters 2 and 3.

Nevertheless, the individual can only achieve so much. If the culture – of department, faculty or division – is not supportive of writing, the individual academic, particularly one who has not published before, may struggle to produce. It helps immensely to have a local 'champion', particularly if he or she actively and visibly supports developing writers:

> When I did my first conference paper (and won a research prize) he congratulated me and encouraged me to publish. He's always following up. Always on email. Always 'in your box'. He reads everyone's papers.

In practice, the person who has already taken on this role is often the one who seeks out or constructs this type of programme or finds other ways to support developing writers.

Structure

While the writing for publication programme has taken many forms, over many years of development and iteration, the model displayed below seems to be one of the most effective. With six meetings over a six-month period, each meeting has a particular focus, but all meetings include the activities listed in the right-hand column. The sequence of topics was designed to lead developing writers through the process of writing a paper, step by step.

Writing for publication programme structure

Topics	Activities at this meeting	. . . at all meetings
Month 1 Writing goal Target journal Support for writing	Writing to prompts Reviewing journals and ideas Discuss with 'writing buddy'	WRITING
Month 2 Target and goal Structure of academic writing	Draft abstract Outline paper	DISCUSSION

Month 3		
New strategies	Freewriting and generative writing	
Criteria and conventions	Analysing published papers	FEEDBACK
Month 4		
Content and argument	Drafting sections	
Giving and receiving feedback	Pre-peer review	PLANNING
Month 5		
Progressing paper	Drafting and revising	MONITORING
Month 6		
Peer review	Analysing reviews and responses	REVISING
Closure	Revising	

At the first meeting, participants are introduced to the structure of the whole programme (see above) and have time to discuss it. They then define and share their writing goals for this programme. This often prompts discussion of the purposes of academic writing – both personal and professional – as participants identify, and weigh in the balance, both internal and external drivers for writing. This discussion may be crucial for participants, as it is one of the moments when they focus on their motivations to write.

The use of 'writing to prompts' (Murray, 2004: 82), a form of adapted freewriting (Elbow, 1973), is helpful at this point in the paper-writing process: it generally stimulates writers to generate potential topics for papers and to recognize that they 'have something to say'. This strategy foregrounds their own ideas, while discussion is balanced by consideration of the context for these ideas, bringing a critical 'edge' to this discussion.

A key initial step, to be taken as early as possible – that is, before, during or shortly after this meeting – is choosing a target journal, since this choice will define each writer's audience and purpose. This step encourages writers to 'think rhetorically, that is, to balance the demands of the subject against [their] own intents and purposes and the needs and expectations of readers' (Rankin, 2001: 51). Thus, this meeting includes discussion of both personal writing goals and the contexts in which these goals may be realized – an important combination that characterizes future meetings.

If participants do drop out of the programme, they tend to do so at this point. While the causes may vary and have multiple sources, it is always a reminder of the need to encourage writers at this stage in their first writing projects. Even if they fall behind, or feel that they have, it is possible to keep them on board. It is neither necessary nor feasible for everyone to progress through the programme at the same rate. From this point on, it is likely that participants will all be at different stages in the paper-writing process. Sometimes this obvious point has to be restated for new writers who, at least initially, may lack confidence.

Between the monthly meetings, participants are encouraged, from the outset, to hold interim meetings, perhaps with a 'writing buddy', in order to progress sub-goals defined at meetings.

At the second meeting, the key writing task, for each participant, is drafting an abstract for the paper, using 'Brown's 8 questions' (Murray, 2004: 111), where writers sketch the main lines of the argument for their papers, from rationale to contribution, and set limits to the contents of their papers. The draft abstract can then be 'calibrated' with the norms and forms of published abstracts in the target journal at the time of writing. This draft abstract will be revised many times, but it serves a useful focusing function at this stage in the writing process. It also helps writers to shape the structure of their papers, another key task for this meeting, as they begin to outline the main sections and sub-sections.

Again, writers have to balance what they want to 'say' in their papers, what their target journals want to 'hear' and to map writing sub-goals in real time. They can also begin to adopt the role of helping each other to define and achieve goals and sub-goals.

It is important to prompt writers – and to encourage them to prompt each other – to produce writing plans for the rest of the programme at this stage. Since every meeting in the programme includes writing time, they can plan to progress their paper in this way, but they are likely to need more time than this. Since writing time is generally not formally allocated, time may have to be made for defined writing tasks. Use of time is an important talking point among writers at this stage, but it is important that this discussion produces a writing timetable, that timetables are reviewed and discussed with peers, and that they are a point of reference when participants talk about their writing both at programme and at interim meetings.

Participants have found it useful to structure interim meetings using the monitoring framework described later in this chapter. This framework is not designed to provide data for management; instead, it works to sharpen writers' focus on their writing sub-goals and to learn to set realistic, incremental goals for writing. For new writers, this is easier said than done, but the programme helps them to adapt their thinking, planning and practices, in light of their experiences and observations.

The third meeting introduces two topics that sustain the dual themes of individual expression and contextualized writing: freewriting (Elbow, 1973) and generative writing (Boice, 1990), two strategies that are usually new to academics, provide modes of developing thinking in writing, build confidence and fluency, and help writers get into the writing habit; by contrast, analysis of published papers often creates a sense of constraint, sometimes inhibition and intimidation, as relatively inexperienced writers recognize the power structures associated with certain topics, methods or writing styles and assess the standard required in their target journals. Discussion at this meeting should almost certainly include these tensions: writing what you want to say, which can be a considerable challenge in itself, and writing in a way that is persuasive to a specific audience. Individual writers must find their own resolutions to the dilemmas these tensions may create. Arguably, these tensions feature in all writing, but new writers often attribute them to deficiencies in their own writing.

The second half of the programme focuses on drafting, revising and peer review. In addition to the above key topics, participants share successful strategies, hints and tips, and compare accounts of the writing process. These narrative accounts are an important dimension of the programme, since they provide specific insights on academic writing and allow participants to individualize their learning.

For further 'tuning' of the programme to suit participants' needs, feedback can be gathered between meetings. For example, in one programme, participants reported at the second meeting on what they had achieved since the first:

> Since the last meeting I have further researched the literature . . . and, in terms of context, the literature on where the subject is going. I have written short review sections on both of these topics, and these will be incorporated into the literature review section of the paper. The time spent has probably been spread over a month. The number of words produced is about 1000, and the sub-themes involved are those indicated above.

These notes, when they are all collected together at the end of the programme, allow participants to look back at their earlier thinking, to view the stages in and pacing of their writing process and to monitor their use of writing subgoals.

For outputs other than journal articles, these processes have been adapted. The pacing of topics, activities and outputs described above has worked well for a range of different academic writing projects. The very different response rates of journals will also influence the pace of publication, and while this is not something they can control, it may affect their choice of target journals.

Early forms of the writing for publication programme consisted of four meetings over six months. Subsequently, in response to participant feedback, this became six meetings over six months. More recently, feedback suggests that even this is not enough. Some find that monthly meetings are too far apart, and suggest that they would benefit from additional meetings to help them reach their interim deadlines. Writers who demand more time may still be learning how to use writing time; they may still be finding out that they cannot do as much as they thought they could in the time available, or that they have to use that time differently. A solution may be to use one or more of the following strategies: writing 'buddies', monitoring meetings and a writing mentor. These support the programme and, above all, progress writing projects.

Writing 'buddies'

Since the last meeting the progress of the writing project has been slow in terms of word output. The current stage of the research is still in the reading stage and the interviews are about to begin. Bearing that in mind I have carried out about four freewriting sessions for approximately 10 mins and have met with my study buddy on 2 occasions. Through these sessions I do have a clearer idea of the structure of the paper but I have to admit it is still in general terms, further clarification and goal setting are required. I feel until these sub-goals are constructed the freewriting and study buddy meetings are not all that constructive. The question arises 'well, what am I going to write about?' The literature section is probably what I should now be concentrating on and again to get output, which to date has only been in scribbled paragraphs. Notwithstanding, a journal has been targeted.

This email shows that the development of a paper, in terms of thinking, reading and inquiry, takes time. Not all meetings or strategies seem 'constructive', and one of the purposes of working with a writing buddy is to keep the project moving forward, working through such 'slow' stages. In addition, relatively inexperienced academic writers tend to forget that they are still learning, and that it takes time to adapt their knowledge and skills to this new task. Working together, they can provide positive feedback on both the process and the emerging product. However, if they are to take up this role, it is useful to have initial briefing and periodic review of the writing buddy role. Clearly, it will not be as helpful to list and analyse inconsistency and incompleteness in a colleague's writing; the writer is likely to be aware of these problems already. Instead, buddies can refer to the WfP framework to adjust their focus. Even inexperienced writers, who may lack confidence in giving feedback on writing, can use the framework as a point of reference for feedback sessions.

In practice, some of these relationships last well beyond the writing programme, suggesting that, in some instances, the relationship has been purposeful and enjoyable. Even when academics come to write their second or third papers, they may still be learning about the academic writing process. For each new journal, there may be differences in the writing they have to produce. In the medium term, buddies can, for example, remind each other of the elements of the programme that worked for them in the past, and, over the longer term, working together, they can adapt the programme's practices to suit their needs.

Perhaps the most important effect of the writing buddy relationship is that the commitment of working with another writer, and knowing that a colleague is committed to writing with you, helps writers make time for writing.

Monitoring meetings

To enhance and develop the 'buddy' approach, more deliberate and structured monitoring can help writers achieve their goals during the WfP programme. Writing buddies and sub-groups have used this framework to structure their interim meetings. The purpose of monitoring meetings is not to provide data for formal review – although writers may use it for that purpose – but to prompt developing writers to use interim meetings as deadlines for sub-goals. The importance of this process is underscored by participants in many programmes who reported that monthly meetings were too far apart.

Monitoring framework

1 To make this process productive, bring the outline of your writing to meetings.
2 To provide writing practice/warm-up, write in sentences.
3 Be specific: number of mins/hours, words written/to write, sub-headings etc.

5 mins' writing	*What writing have you done on your project since the previous meeting?*
10 mins' writing	*Write about the next theme/heading/topic on your writing agenda.*
10 mins' discussion	*Discuss what you wrote with your partner/group.*
5 mins' writing	*What is your next sub-goal for your writing project?*

This approach – and particularly these questions – may seem to go against the 'non-surveillance' ethos of other strategies described in this book, such as writers' retreat, but it depends on how it is managed: is it a 'mini research assessment exercise', focusing on 'hard' output, or are participants monitoring 'soft' outcomes, such as growing confidence, reduced anxiety associated with writing, or writing-in-progress outputs? Although the emphasis in many academic and research contexts is on the former, it is important, particularly for first-time writers, to focus on the latter. This is not to say that outputs are unimportant; quite the reverse, the monitoring framework encourages writers to establish outputs for every meeting and to see what they can learn from monitoring their outputs.

In order to prepare writers for this role, self- and peer-monitoring are built into the WfP programme. Part of each meeting is spent taking stock of the extent to which writers achieved the goals they set themselves at the previous meeting, along with the setting and resetting of goals to be achieved by the next meeting.

A writing mentor

Like the writing 'buddy', a writing mentor can support the developing writer throughout the writing process. Those with responsibility for research mentoring can add the stages in the writing process to their discussions with writers. This may be a new interpretation of the mentor's role, and may present a new challenge to many mentors: 'As I'm talking, I'm learning at the same time.'

These words probably best capture the approach of an effective writing mentor. Certainly the person who said them was, according to evaluations of one programme, an effective writing mentor, but these words also remind us that while some people are able mentors in one role, becoming a writing mentor may make new demands. In some institutions new mentors have met with a coordinator or in groups, or shared issues and strategies by email, in order to review their experiences in this new role and to learn from each other.

One of the main challenges for writing mentors may be making time for their role:

> I am one of the writing mentors . . . I'm sorry, but I won't be able to attend the group tomorrow – an emergency meeting has been called in my department.

Another challenge for writing mentors is motivating writers in the early stages of their first projects:

> I'm sorry I won't be able to come because I need some motivation top-up! One of my group has dropped out. I was in weekly contact with the other two about writing, and one did give me something to read. But I haven't done much at all since then. I think that it becomes difficult, maybe off-putting, when there's not much sign of progress. I'm not sure how much to push, and I'm all too sympathetic to the problems of writing.

The response of the person coordinating the WfP programme in which this mentor was working highlights the need for using the principles of the programme to structure the mentor's role:

> In answer to your questions: the writers have goals for the next few weeks and months, and it would be useful if you discussed with them – face-to-face or by email – how they are progressing towards their goals and any blocks that come up. One thing you can stress is that it is too early to see

changes in their practices and outputs. So you could include a reminder to set achievable goals and to give positive feedback as small steps are taken. It might be useful to help your group identify failed goals, but probably important to end on a positive note. Do this now, before writing gets pushed into the background again.

This response highlights a key role for writing mentors: making writing a topic of regular discussion. This is one way of keeping it 'in the foreground', that is, helping writers they are mentoring to prioritize writing. In other words, the mentor is not there to check up on writers, but to supply encouragement, positive feedback and a sounding board for writing problems. While many new writing mentors do not feel equipped to solve 'writing problems', they can prompt writers to adopt the strategies covered in this chapter and in the rest of this book. Using the six-month programme outlined in this chapter helps mentors to align their role with stages writers are working through.

The following outline of the writing mentor's role provides an initial guide. Derived from experiences with many groups of writers, its purpose is to prompt discussion among those learning to play the role and those who have experience as writing mentors.

The writing mentor's role

Remit

The mentor supports writers between meetings in the writing for publication programme. More specifically, the role involves the following:

- supporting the development of specific, achievable goals and sub-goals and maintaining writers' focus on them;
- maintaining contact with writers in the programme in meetings or emails;
- providing support and advice to writers as required;
- monitoring writers' progress towards achieving specified goals;
- monitoring 'writing buddy' and other mentoring relationships;
- encouraging writers to monitor themselves;
- following up drop-outs from the programme.

Experience suggests that different writers require different forms of support; that is, all of these forms will not be required by all writers in the programme. In addition, the role can be customized by writers and mentors.

Tasks

The mentor's activities will probably include the following:

- weekly email contact with writers;
- occasional one-to-one discussions as required;
- occasional discussions with sub-groups of two to four writers.

If appropriate and with permission: the mentor can log interactions with writers in order to provide tracking data, in addition to final data, for evaluation of the programme.

Time

The time commitment for mentors is approximately 15 minutes per week, or 30 minutes every two weeks, per writer.

This is not just about mentors reading final versions of papers, but about them being part of the writing process. This may be challenging, even for experienced writers acting as mentors. Even more challenging may be acting as a mentor while still being an inexperienced writer, yet there have been cases in which new writers have played a mentoring role for other new writers. The above framework will help those who are prepared to transfer their mentoring skills to this context.

There have, of course, been instances where the mentoring role was not effective, where the mentor had too many other responsibilities, where the interpersonal dynamic was not positive or where mentoring meetings, for a variety of reasons, did not seem purposeful. In these cases, it is difficult to know what writers and mentors can learn; it is difficult to measure the impact of so many variables, and, since the approach is relatively new, it may be premature to analyse the problem on the basis of such limited data.

A key role for mentors is helping writers to identify differences between assumptions about academic writing and actual writing practices. If mentors can prompt writers to identify their own successful and unsuccessful practices, they will save them a considerable amount of trial and error. Group discussions among writers should make it clear that there are various routes to writing, even in the same discipline, but writers can be side-tracked by comparing their modest progress with an expected output that may be unrealistic. Mentors can help writers to focus on what they have achieved simply by asking them and pointing out the extent to which they have achieved the goals they set themselves. Mentors can also support writers who are members of a writers' group, the subject of the next chapter.

Evaluations

Even when participants were interviewed one year or more after completing the programme, their feedback tends to be very positive. Evaluations and findings from small-scale evaluation studies suggest that those who complete the programme experience a number of benefits in behavioural, cognitive and affective domains:

New discussions

- 'hearing others' experiences of and viewpoints on writing'
- 'giving a more collective reference point'
- 'reassuring . . . in that it has opened up the topic and dispelled some of the taboos about the whole process'
- 'felt less isolated'
- 'let me see that I'm not alone, neither am I very far behind'.

New priorities

- 'the W*f*P [writing for publication] programme has put the process of writing onto a formal agenda'
- 'had to allocate time to attend meetings'

New behaviours

- 'changes in participants' behaviour over the course'
- 'writing in "bite-sized chunks"'
- 'setting aside time for writing'
- 'much more organized and managed process'

New attitudes

- 'more positive in my attitude to writing'

New knowledge

- 'analysing published writing'

New culture

- 'Will help consolidate a research culture'

This is not to say that all W*f*P programmes produced all these impacts for all participants; however, these responses, together with the fact that even those who attended only part of a W*f*P programme were equally positive, suggests that the programme can be of benefit. Moreover, the duration of the W*f*P programme means that participants were able to comment on changes that occurred in their writing before – sometimes well before – the programme ended.

In addition, there is evidence that output increases: 'It is difficult to assess, but my guess is [the W*f*P programme has] doubled output', was how one research coordinator who had participated in the programme measured its impact on 'hard' output.

While the W*f*P programme has many potentially beneficial effects, there is evidence that it only takes writers so far. For the duration of the programme, the recurring problem of making writing time was solved for participating writers. When the programme ended, however, writers had to find new ways to make regular writing time slots. In order to become regular writers, they had to establish a writing schedule: 'By allocating to writing a specific daily or weekly time slot, a schedule ensures that you will get to do it on a regular basis' (Zerubavel, 1999: 5).

An ideal way of consolidating the effects of the programme and solving the 'time' problem is a writers' group – the subject of the next chapter. In many ways, and for many writers, a writers' group provides the essential follow-on from a W*f*P programme. It maintains the academic writer's focus on process, one of the key benefits of the programme: 'The biggest impact has been on process. The freewriting approach has freed my writing style and I am now more able to write at length without interruption by other activities.' More importantly, it helps writers to maintain this focus on their writing processes, when the focus of other initiatives is so often exclusively on the finished product.

Checklist

- Think about what the stages in your writing process are or could be.
- Decide on your writing goal – if it's writing a paper, choose a journal.
- Set up a series of meetings over six months with a group of other writers.
- Make it a formal programme: put 'meetings' in your diary and book a room.
- Write when you meet – don't just talk about writing.
- Consider finding a facilitator to provide new strategies and information.
- Consider pros and cons of writing 'buddies' – for discussions and feedback.

7

Writers' groups

Introduction • The purpose of writers' groups • How does a writers' group work? • Making time to write • Providing 'pre-peer review' • Taking the sting out of peer review • Checklist for writers' groups

Introduction

This chapter describes how a writers' group can help academics already engaged in writing for publication to develop productive strategies and continue to generate published outputs. It does this in two ways: firstly, by applying peer review in the earlier stages of writing and, secondly, by subjecting the process – not just the product – of academic writing to the rigour of peer review. Along with this rigour, it must be emphasized that participating academics report that a writers' group is one of the most collegial environments that they have experienced.

The contents of this chapter are underpinned by our experience of running and participating in different types of writers' groups in universities and other institutions in several countries over more than a decade. From their discussions and evaluations, we extracted principles of good practice and identified difficulties academics say they face in achieving it.

Ongoing, active speculation about academic writing may be a sensible approach for academics to take, particularly those who are still developing their skills in this area. Moreover, like the writing for publication programme, a writers' group approach is not for everyone, but issues raised in writers' group discussions and evaluations often shed light on problems academic writers face and the range of individual solutions they find, sometimes quite quickly, in the writers' group context.

In this chapter we present principles and practices observed over time, recurring in writers' discussions, cutting across different educational and disciplinary cultures, and for which there was evidence of immediate and/or lasting impact (Murray and MacKay, 1998; Grant and Knowles, 2000; Morss and Murray, 2001; Lee and Boud, 2003; Moore, 2003).

The purpose of writers' groups

Why should academics 'need' a writers' group? What is its purpose? These questions are often asked by academics who already experience 'group' effects in their writing in their departments. For example, in some academic departments, researchers work in groups to progress reading and/or writing. In these contexts, writers' group may be seen as redundant. However, in some disciplines these benefits are not available, and for academics to benefit from a group effect, they must set up groups themselves, either in departments, or with colleagues in other departments.

For those who see writing as an activity usually performed in solitude, a group approach can seem strange. Academics who have not seen a writers' group at work are often curious to know how they could write 'in a group'. Many assume that it would be distracting to write in the same place as other writers, and that feedback from colleagues in other disciplines would have little relevance. Most of all, they fear that it would be a waste of one of their most precious resources – time. Why not just 'get on with the writing?', is a question asked of writers' group participants by non-participating academics.

As with the other interventions we have described there may also be a fear of being stigmatized as someone who 'needs help with writing'. There may be a view – or a fear that someone will take the view – that a writers' group is a remedial intervention for those whose work is not up to scratch. There is debate about whether the processes we describe in this chapter are already available in 'good' academic departments and performed by 'good' academics. We acknowledge that these processes could and perhaps should be provided in 'good' academic departments – though we know that, in many cases, they are not. We are less concerned with the debate about where and how writing skills 'should' be developed and more concerned about providing frameworks for academics to develop their writing. This is the purpose of a writers' group: not simply to increase 'outputs' but also to find ways to improve practices.

How does a writers' group work?

There are many ways to run writers' groups, and the format probably has to be flexible and responsive, as does each participant, until you establish how you all want to work, who is committed to writing in this way and so on. Since the best way to learn about how a writers' group works is to try it, this section explains the approach briefly, providing enough information and advice to get started. (For more detail, see Murray, 2004.) Once you have established your group, you can adapt the approach to suit yourselves.

Elements of a writers' group

Principles

Based on our work with academic writers' groups over the past ten years, we propose, as a starting point, that there are three underpinning principles:

1 Writing is a social act that benefits from discussion with peers.
2 Feedback can be helpful at different stages in the writing process.
3 Working in a group can motivate writers to initiate and progress projects and produce successful outputs.

Alternatively, you may identify different principles, or your group may value one of these over the others, or you may develop others after you meet. It might be as well to discuss this explicitly at the outset, to see if you agree, or agree to disagree. You could use our three principles as a starting point for your discussion.

Note: writers' group differs from other forms of group work where there is a common group goal. Unless you are writing collaboratively, you are in the group to progress an individual goal, and this may affect participants differently.

Participants

A university writers' group can be a self-selecting group of academics, perhaps from different disciplines.

Facilitator/chair

This should be someone who can chair discussions, prompt group members to articulate views, move them on from discussion to writing, keep discussion focused on projects and prompt a problem-solving approach to writing barriers. Anyone who is willing to chair your group will do in the first instance, or you may find that your 'group' consists of three or four regulars, hardly requiring a 'chair'. Alternatively, in the knowledge that many peer groups work well without chairs, you may decide to go ahead without one, in order not to put off starting.

Practices

While it is important to be flexible and responsive in managing writers' group meetings, our experience suggests that there are three core elements:

1   Participants identify a specific writing project from the outset.
2   All meetings include writing time, goal setting and peer discussion.
3   Participants discuss both what they write and how they write.

We alert you to new participants' inclination simply to discuss their writing and to defer the writing itself, thus missing opportunities to write. Writers' group meetings are likely to seem purposeful if writing is progressed, that is actually produced, during meetings. We reassure new writers that while writing during meetings may seem odd at first, it quickly becomes routine. Broadly speaking, there are two types of writing that you can usefully do in writers' group: (1) writing about writing, which acts as a focusing and 'warm-up' activity and (2) writing for the project, in which, for example, you choose a topic from your outline or abstract and write a section of the paper.

What do you write about?

Writing about writing

1   What is your writing project?
2   What stage is the project at?
3   What is your next writing task?
4   What is your immediate writing task/topic for today's meeting?

Writing/drafting the project

1   The purpose of this section is to . . .
2   Begin writing a section of your outline.
3   Write sentences that define the purpose of your sections/sub-sections.
4   Write sentences to follow/explicate/develop these.

The writing-about-writing tasks can be done in 5 minutes, while the writing-for-the-project tasks should be allocated much more time, for example 30 to 50 minutes.

Timings

Meetings typically last between 60 and 90 minutes and are held once or twice a month. Alternatively, you might find that you have as little as 30 minutes or as much as two hours in any given week or month, and you may decide to vary the timing to suit. Fixing a time for writers' group meetings can itself be time-consuming. Rather than using up time at the end of meetings looking for a date, it may be quicker to set a regular day and time.

These are the parameters, but every group develops its own rhythms, goals and norms. The most important thing is, of course, to make sure that the group focuses on writing, stimulates participants to write – outlining, drafting or revising – and helps them to produce their intended outputs. New groups can monitor their experiences by discussing these issues and outputs, and such discussions can be hugely revealing and highly instructive. They can also provide valuable peer review on writing-in-progress.

Each group can reflect on and learn from its experiences. It is probably important, therefore, to make time to review the group's activities and participants' perceptions of its usefulness from time to time.

Whatever your position in the debate about how academic writers learn to do what they do (Hartley and Branthwaite, 1989), we suggest that a writers' group can provide crucial support at key moments in your writing career. Our experience suggests that a writers' group supports academic writing through three main functions:

1 Making time to write.
2 Providing 'pre-peer review'.
3 Taking the sting out of peer review.

Because participants in many groups identified these as key benefits, we focus on them in this chapter, with particular emphasis on the last: because negative peer review can cause academics to stop writing for publication, this is the subject of the longest section.

Making time to write

The factor most commonly cited by academics as a reason for not writing is 'time'. This problem is alleviated by a writers' group because it allows participants to prioritize and legitimize writing time during working hours, not just in personal time.

For example, a group could meet on Friday afternoons, every two weeks, so that it becomes routine. In this way, writers' group meetings come to be regarded like other regular meetings. This helps writers to stop moving writing time around to make time for other tasks, and start to find ways of moving other tasks around, so as to make time for writing: 'I am trying to move classes to allow me to attend the writers' group meeting on Wednesday and will confirm by Monday.'

This option is not available to everyone, but a writers' group can help participants to consider their options. Nor was the writer quoted above immune to the ambivalence of the decision he made, as he revealed some time later: 'every activity that is related to teaching students has, in my mind, a higher priority than the writing'. These tensions can be resolved in writers' group discussions. Academics can change their attitude to their writing and their approaches to doing it in a writers' group.

For example, some academics state they are too tired to write on a Friday afternoon, yet we have known several groups to run at this time, over a number of years, to good effect. Participants regularly report that while they arrive at their writers' group feeling exhausted and demoralized, they leave feeling energized.

Once they are meeting regularly to write in this way, participants report that they shift from finding themselves too stretched and stressed to write to being relieved when writers' group meetings come around, or, as one participant put it: 'I'm hanging on by my fingernails here. Writers' group is the only thing that's keeping me going.' This writer was at that point in the academic year when his teaching load was at its heaviest: with hundreds of scripts to mark and dozens of meetings with students, he had no time for writing. From his perspective, the writers' group not only 'created' two hours, every two weeks, for writing, it also let him go some way towards achieving a personal priority – writing for academic journals – while still meeting other commitments.

Without entering into the debate about what an inability to make time for a priority is 'really' about, we can say that a writers' group provides not only a forum for writers to engage with this question, but also a solution to the problem. This is not to say that a writers' group resolves time-tabling tensions, but it does seem that group effects help writers shift the locus of control: they begin to find ways of breaking the 'time barrier' to writing.

Since a writers' group provides short writing time slots, it allows participants to try this new mode, to discuss its pros and cons, and to perceive its effect in practice.

A writers' group also helps academics set better writing goals and experience satisfaction when they achieve them. The recurring phenomenon of writers reporting that they have done 'very little' between group meetings, when they have done more than they set out to do, may indicate that academics are setting themselves unachievable goals, or it may tell us that they are

---

About time

- Keep an open mind about how time 'should' be used for writing.
- Articulate your views and practices on 'writing time'.
- Engage with other writers' views and practices.
- Share and compare constructively.
- Use both long and short writing time slots.
- Write in ways that don't initially 'feel right'.
- Look for ways to change how you make writing time.
- Learn from other writers in your group.
- Find out how productive writers make time to write.
- Make a regular writing time slot.
- Use writers' group meetings as deadlines.
- Articulate, discuss and note changes in your use of time.
- Record the writers' group on your *curriculum vitae* and annual review.

not good at measuring their progress in terms of their goals. This is why a key function of a writers' group is setting interim goals, or sub-goals, at each meeting.

In practice, writers' group discussions often involve the 'resetting' of writing goals, as participants help each other establish feasible goals and time slots for achieving them. This may take more confidence than new writers have. It also requires participants to reposition what seems like a 'failed' goal to a reset goal. A writers' group is therefore a forum where academics learn about goal setting for writing from each other, and their own goal-setting strategies. That these must adapt, if the academic is to make time to write, is part of the work of the writers' group for each individual. Only by reviewing your goals can you learn these lessons, specific to your writing and to the real contexts in which you write.

You can learn about this from the literature, but activation and practice are needed before new knowledge affects your writing. You can read the literature on goal setting and improve your understanding of writing goals, but you can learn much more from monitoring your own practice. The goals are not always the same for everything you write. For example, you may find that you write different papers in different ways, and that these differences may have to do with how you balance other tasks at different points in the academic year. Alternatively, you may find that you do all your best writing at the same point in the year, and your task is then to ensure that you have some protected time at that point, year on year.

A writers' group prompts you to take a good look at how you use time and how you set an achievable goal for the duration of writers' group meetings or for the period between meetings. While in the short term a writers' group helps you make time to write, over the longer term it helps you find additional writing time.

Providing 'pre-peer review'

While peer review occurs after you finish a writing project, for example, when you submit a paper to a journal, pre-peer review occurs earlier, for example, when you are developing your paper, at the drafting stage and just before submission. The purpose of pre-peer review is to help you anticipate critiques, strengthen your paper and build your confidence:

> So what of the confidence that is necessary to produce a paper for publication? Here we have a problem of committing ideas and views to paper and exposing them to a wide audience. Furthermore, that audience will include people who have extensive knowledge of the subject of the paper and may disagree with the views expressed.

Pre-peer review can either be oral or in writing, and the type of discussion it generates can help writers in a number of different ways:

- You can rehearse arguments and counter-arguments, helping each other to anticipate refutations and strengthen your arguments.
- You can develop a positive view of your own writing-in-progress. When academics talk about the difficult stages in the academic writing process, they use words like 'messy', 'unfocused', 'clumsy', 'rough' and even 'chaotic'; in a writers' group, you may still use these terms, but they will have a more precise, less emotive, meaning. You see the stages in writing process, and the challenges that each presents.
- You begin to 'smooth' the hard-edged judgements that academics often make of their own writing, shifting your focus from the gaps and deficiencies in what you have written to the next revision.

A writers' group helps you review your conception of writing problems:

> There are many obstacles to the writing process. These include priorities of work and home life, inappropriate conditions for writing and the inability to get started. The greatest difficulty for me personally is in overcoming the need to have the . . . paper fully researched, planned and a framework set out prior to starting to write.

This writer explodes the myth that having an outline – and the other strategies he mentions – is the key to writing papers. In a writers' group, academics can voice their views on writing, define writing problems and prompt each other to find solutions. One year later, this writer demonstrated the type of conceptual shift and significant behavioural change that a writers' group brings about:

> I have now moved away from the need for completion of research prior to writing. Writing and research are iterative. Regular writing is necessary to direct the next part of the research. Regular writing is also necessary as a measure of progress.

This is one example of the kinds of change that a writers' group helps academics to make. Whether that change takes one year or one month will depend on the individual writer and, perhaps, on the group.

It is not the purpose of this chapter to prescribe one way for you to give and receive feedback in your writers' group. You and your colleagues will develop a collection of comments to make at different stages. Over time, you will notice patterns in outputs and feedback. You may develop group and individual repertoires for feedback on writing-in-progress. Once you unpack, describe and analyse stages in the writing process, you find out what constitutes effective feedback.

As a starting point, think about some basic briefing (see also Chapter 3.) As for other aspects of a writers' group, these are processes that we find work with different groups, but you may develop your own.

Briefing your readers

- Tell them what stage your writing is at.
- Tell them what feedback you'd like.
- Identify to them the part of your text (not all) you want feedback on.

Giving feedback

- Try listening without interacting – thus not controlling the discussion.
- Highlight the best feature first.

So as to help your readers get a sense of whether or not what they say to you is useful, it is a good idea to have a brief discussion after they have given you their feedback.

Debriefing your readers

- Identify the point(s) that you found useful.
- Say what you learned from the feedback.
- Describe any changes you will make/have made to your writing.
- Any changes you will make when asking for feedback next time?
- Any changes your colleague will make when giving you feedback again?

You may, for example, think that your colleague did not give you the feedback you asked for. Before you go any further, you might want to discuss that. You may find that they are well aware of this, and that they had their own views on what is needed in your writing, and this, again, reveals the different understandings of many aspects of writing. This articulation of different views is one of the most interesting aspects of a writers' group.

Some will argue that this is 'just more talk' when again you should 'just get on with the writing'. Another view is that such discussion makes you aware of issues you might not have previously considered. It may also save you and your peers time in the future. If the feedback is considered in this way, your colleague is more likely to give up time to read your writing again. This discussion also consolidates your commitment to advancing your writing project in specific ways, and the more specific, the easier it is to make time for them.

At some point you may have to prompt your reviewer to give you more rigorous feedback, to ask harder questions:

- 'What do you mean by . . .?'
- 'There seems to be a bit of a jump here . . .'
- 'How does that relate to your main point?'
- 'Where is your evidence for . . .?'

Not every academic will immediately see how he or she can give feedback on a paper in another discipline. However, cross-disciplinary feedback sessions have proved extremely productive. For example, scientists and social scientists reading each other's work will not be 'in tune' with each other's methodology, and may define 'rigour' differently. Where the scientist will not make a claim without evidence or reference, a social scientist has more space to speculate. This generalization may seem too sweeping, and it is not our intention to stereotype the disciplines, but the example is taken from writers' discussions.

There is merit in working in interdisciplinary groups. Having to make a case for your methodology, for example, helps you to articulate and justify what you did, and this conversation may function as another 'rehearsal' for your writing. On the other hand, that rehearsal may be very different, expressed in quite different terms, from the terms you want to use in your paper. Nevertheless, we cannot with confidence assert that this would have negative effects. That itself would be difficult to evidence, and it may be more sensible to conclude that, since participants in some writers' groups have found this process very helpful, others might too. This takes us back to our repeated injunction to you to try this for yourself, in order to see how it works for you and your colleagues. In our groups, some of those who were initially sceptical about how useful feedback from colleagues in other disciplines could be came to see it as more useful than feedback in their own disciplines.

Alternatively, it could be damaging if there is a 'language barrier' between the disciplines, or if one writer assumes the superiority of one discipline, in terms of rigour, for example, over another, or if there is an apparent lack of respect expressed about the work that is the subject of the writing. For a writers' group to work, there must be a culture of trust, a sense that the group is collegial and friendly, and a spirit of debate and intellectual inquiry. When these features are in place, participants can relax in peer review, rather than finding it intimidating.

Of course, there will be writers' groups that include academics from the same 'family' of disciplines. In this instance, even when there are wide philosophical and/or methodological variations, discussions can create stimulating connections and potential synergies, thus developing the research culture.

Analysis of academic writing, as discussed in the previous chapter, can be conducted and continued in a writers' group. Writers' group discussion increases our awareness of styles and practices that will help us to produce writing of the highest standard regularly.

Pre-peer review prepares you for peer review, which can be more daunting, challenging and even destructive. If you have been through several debates about your writing-in-progress and have had feedback from peers, then not only should the paper you submit be stronger, but you should be prepared for the kinds of questions journal reviewers ask and quicker to see solutions to problems they identify in your writing.

Taking the sting out of peer review

We devote space in this chapter to this topic because of the power that reviews have to motivate and inhibit academic writing: we know academics who stopped writing after they received negative or destructive reviews from journals. While there may have been additional factors at work in that decision, it is reasonable to say that peer review can 'sting' and may be unfair or uneven:

> Referees are not always consistent in what they recommend . . . Different referees have different opinions . . . And there is much research on the reliability and validity of this 'peer review' system.
>
> (Hartley, 2005: 16)

Yet, however many questions we have about the consistency, reliability and validity of reviewers' comments, we can learn from peer review to improve our writing: there is evidence that the review process raises the quality of papers (Lock, 1986; Weller, 2001; Fletcher and Fletcher, 2003), and the sooner we work out how reviews can improve our writing the better. One way of doing this is to bring reviews to a writers' group, in order to analyse reviewers' comments and work out how to revise the paper.

It could be argued that if your research is weak and your writing is poor, you should stop writing for publication and focus on other academic roles. However, it is the contention of this chapter that development and support in a writers' group can help academics make best use of peer reviews to improve their writing. It can also help them overcome the initial shock and resentment they may feel and to shift their perspective from 'reviewee' to 'writer'.

This section describes how writers' groups can help you work through and learn from even the most destructive review. While some reviewers' comments are negative to the point of being destructive, it is important to move beyond emotional reactions to negative reviews and to scrutinize interpretations of them. While in a writers' group we may use negative terms about our writing-in-progress, it is a different matter when other academics use them to describe our writing. In a writers' group you can debate interpretations of a reviewer's comments, work out where the reviewer is coming from, which position he or she is taking in the debate you have entered in your paper, and discuss different ways of revising your writing in order to accommodate those different positions, without losing the essence or impact of what you want to say. In some cases, this is a fine balancing act that benefits from detailed discussion with peers.

To illustrate these points, we analyse three reviews received by three authors in three different disciplines. The recipients of the reviews granted us permission to do so, but we altered details in order to preserve their anonymity; nor do we seek to identify the reviewers, and we therefore do not specify the journals involved. These examples could be the subject of writers' group discussion, perhaps followed by discussion of participants' own reviews.

After many discussions with colleagues – both new and experienced writers – we decided to quote selected comments from the reviews, so as to convey their full impact. Had we summarized the reviews we would, at least, have removed some of their sting, and, at worst, failed to define some of the features of destructive reviews and, more importantly, strategies for coping with and acting on them.

This is not to say that all peer reviews are negative, for they are not; instead, the purpose of this discussion is to illustrate how much excellent work can be achieved through writers' group analyses of critiques. In all three examples, the terms of the critique are highlighted in bold.

Peer review: example 1

I have **serious doubts** about the suitability of this paper to the proposed special issue of [journal title]. My first question is whether this falls within the category of [this area] at all, even loosely defined. Its central concern is with discursive traditions. Discourse analysis is conducted within psychology but carried out in a manner that adds to our understanding of psychological processes. **This is not the case here**. Significantly, the bibliography contains **no** psychology **references**. Secondly, even if the paper could be deemed to be one in political psychology, it is **very thin at the level of substance**. The discussion of the philosophical roots of [the subject] (going back to Cicero) is not without interest, but it is **not particularly illuminating** about contemporary [subject] which – to put it mildly – has been shaped by rather more than a philosophical tradition. The overall impression is of an analysis that is **very remote from its subject matter**. Thirdly, it is not until page 10 of a 17 page paper that the paper gets to the discourses that are its main focus. At that point there is **so little space left to say much** about any of them. I did **not** find the discursive themes to be **particularly revealing**. More concrete examples would have helped. I do **not** think this paper would **make a substantial contribution** to the special issue of the journal.

The temptation, particularly for new writers, is to focus on the negative terms, although these, by themselves, do not give the writer much information:

'serious doubts . . . very thin at the level of substance . . . not particularly illuminating . . . analysis that is very remote from its subject matter . . . so little space left to say much . . . not . . . particularly revealing . . . not . . . make a substantial contribution'

These terms do not help the writer to define specific weaknesses, and such comments are too wide-ranging. Moreover, a writer who focuses on these terms, as many seem to do when they first receive negative reviews or rejections, is not going to be particularly motivated. 'Serious' suggests major weakness, but does not strike all writers as a major criticism. In fact, some writers consider that it is inevitable that reviewers will have questions that lead to 'serious doubts'. The question for the writer is how to address these doubts, whether they can be integrated in the paper itself, without losing its focus, whether this should occur early in the paper, to engage with or even forestall growing 'doubts', or nearer the end, to acknowledge the 'debatability' of the conclusions drawn from the work. This is precisely the focus of writers' group discussion, moving writers from emotional reaction to analytical work, focusing on strengthening the paper, whether that be prior to resubmission or for a new submission.

The writer who received this review remarked that while it had seemed very negative at the time, 'on looking at it again after a long period – is not as awful as I remembered it to be' and then reflected on that shift in her perception:

> Maybe that says something about sensitivity on first opening the letter, and the need to allow a bit of time to elapse before replying. Also developing one's own writing skills and confidence. I think I would be more sanguine about [this] reviewer's comments now than I was at the time.

Writers' group discussion can help you move to this 'sanguine' point without letting so much time elapse. It can help you generate options, as reviser of your own writing, and may help you to modulate your writing so that you do not draw so much fire the next time you submit a paper to a journal. This is not to say that you have to 'take the sting' out of your paper, play safe or never put your head above the parapet; instead, it may mean that you enter the existing debate by both aligning your work with others' and distinguishing yours from theirs.

For example, we have noticed that new writers sometimes overstate either their critique of previous work or their claim to 'contribution'. In a writers' group – if that was not spotted in the 'pre-peer review' stage – you can discuss reviewers' comments with this in mind. In discussing reviews, you are likely to draw up your own list of common errors, along with strategies for avoiding them. Without a writers' group, you have only your own view, perhaps with one or two colleagues, who may not allocate time for such in-depth discussion and may not have been involved in discussions with you as you wrote your paper.

Writers' group discussion lets you find out about reviews that others have received, how they reacted and how they responded. You find out that both positive and negative reviewing occurs in all disciplines, and that you are certainly not the first, or the last, to receive a negative review. Interestingly, discussions of bad reviews often reveal that eminent people receive them – and expect them. While this is hearsay – in the absence of a data set – it helps to know that it is not just your writing that attracts this response.

The second example is a review of a book proposal. The review ran to several pages, but the comments selected here are those the author marked as the ones she found particularly discouraging. Critical terms are marked in bold here in order to focus on problems identified.

Peer review: example 2

There is **no evidence** that the assumptions [the author] makes about the needs and experiences of her student audience actually engage with those of overseas students. The author cites **no information** about the characteristics of the global market and how these compare with the UK one that she aims to cater for. . . .

I suspect **it will be difficult to address adequately** the needs of different postgraduate groups within one book. The current proposal **does not indicate** that [the author] can do this and a new proposal would need to be submitted for review. . . .

I have **serious concerns** about [the author's] approach. . . .

The outline and the sample chapter confirm for me that the book speaks from a **very narrow** base of experience to a very particular group of . . . students. Although the author has clearly experience of part-time postgraduate study as a student and course administrator, this experience base is very limited. . . . There is **no evidence** that the author has **any research** on [the subject] . . . to draw upon to inform her book. There is also **no evidence** that the author's advice is informed by relevant literature. . . .

The circumstances and needs of different groups of part-time students appear to be **completely neglected**. . . .

The proposal and sample chapter **fail to satisfy** me that this is a book that offers something distinctive. . . .

What was most upsetting about this review, when the author first read it, was the repeated use of the word 'no', which seemed overstated, along with the word 'fail'. If she had provided literally 'no' evidence, her proposal would indeed have been seriously weak. The strength, and repetition, of negatives apparently ignores the possibility that there is some, but perhaps not sufficient, use of evidence in her writing. In addition, the words 'narrow' and 'fail' are equally damning. What can an author make of this? What are the options?

- Collect more evidence and provide it in writing.
- Make a stronger case for the evidence supplied.
- State the purpose of limiting the evidence provided.
- Give more detail of evidence – perhaps on one aspect only.
- Align the argument/proposal with others, in terms of evidence supplied.
- Strengthen the case for the sufficiency of the evidence to make the point.

- Acknowledge problems with limited evidence and address them.
- Point to where evidence is supplied elsewhere or by others. Or replace it with a more precise term for what you have, such as 'indications'?
- Distinguish more explicitly what you can and cannot evidence.
- Offset weak evidence with other strengths.

In other words, the writer's options include strengthening the work, the writing or both. By focusing on these issues, writers' group discussion generates a wide range of options, supports the writer who feels that the work is under attack and, more importantly, saves valuable time – the writer proceeds with revisions without the need for an extended 'cooling off' period.

Writers' group participants are likely to have more than one interpretation of reviewers' comments and more than one option for revision. In this instance, analysis can remove some of the initial 'sting' of the negatives. Although this proposal was rejected, it need not be the end of writing about its subject – a proposal can be adapted for other publishers – as long as the author can find different ways to write about it and, more importantly, can summon the motivation to do so.

Example 3 may seem, on first reading, to be the exception: how can the author take any learning points from this review?

Peer review: example 3

. . . I would be reluctant to send my staff to [an event] organized by the author, whose **writing skills are appalling**. . . . The **very ugly jargon** is so pervasive that I have not marked it.

The writing is also **prolix and repetitive**, and thus the article is **far too long**. It is so **loosely organized** that it is hard, when going back to the article, to know where to look for some of the results and comments. . . . But a **fundamental weakness** is the claim in both the abstract and the body of the article that the research 'provides evidence of increased output'. . . . There is **no evidence** that the [event] led to a subsequent increase in [activity] . . .

I don't consider that this article should be published. The irony of a [lecturer] producing such **terrible prose** would be embarrassing. Even if the prose were improved, and the article considerably shortened and better organized, it is **difficult to see what it adds to our knowledge** . . . I find it rather astonishing that such tuition is required – how did these staff get good first degrees and then higher degrees? If any further help is required in shaping an article, does not the head of the department provide this for junior staff?

This example was discussed in several writers' groups, where reactions ranged from shock, to expletive, from 'This review is intemperate' to 'This is so slack . . . and gauche. . . .. The level of rigour is not there in the review itself'. For the author of the paper, this discussion was therapeutic; and without further analysis this might, in itself, be a sufficient argument for a writers' group.

However, another important outcome of these discussions was the broadening of perspective: this writer was not alone in receiving this type of review. This is not the only type of negative review that academics should expect to receive, nor is it true that nothing can be learned from even destructive reviews.

Types of feedback in negative reviews

- Non-specific, but scathing;
- scathing, but useful;
- damning with faint praise (rejection);
- redirecting (to another journal);
- editorial (grammar, punctuation, etc.);
- inviting revision and resubmission.

A writers' group is, of course, not the only way to process negative feedback; any peer group may have similar impact, but the strength of a writers' group is its focus on getting published and continuing to write. Discussion moves on to how the writer can shape the paper for another journal, for example, rather than getting bogged down in debates about injustice or power. Over time – and perhaps in less time than the writer who files negative reviews for a month or more – writers' groups can develop a broader, less personalized perspective on negative reviews, while recognizing that bad reviews still sting.

Levels of response to peer review

Emotional response Depression . . . embarrassment . . . anger
Analytical response 'What can I learn from this?'
Strategic response 'Don't waste a word' – find another journal and rework.

For example 3, there are lessons the writer can learn:

- The writing really *is* 'appalling'.
- Claim to contribution is overstated.
- The structure needs work.
- Alternative views on the subject/work must be added to this paper.

- The rationale for the work must be stronger.
- Another type of paper about this work would be better.
- This paper should go to another journal.

This analysis of three reviews is intended to show how the process of sharing negative reviews provides some of the key benefits of a writers' group. It can quickly direct you to the position some writers only reach after months, working on their own.

At the very least, through a writers' group you make regular time for writing, create regular discussions of your writing and give and receive feedback on writing before submission. You can use a writers' group as a forum for talking about individual processes, processes that you are actually using, or planning to use. Such discussion is not only theoretical, but is based on actual practice. Through this individualization, you can make your group purposeful, but it also raises the question of the relevance of one writer's difficulties to other writers in the group, and that too, like other topics addressed in this chapter, could be an important subject for writers' group discussion.

Once you have created regular time, you may decide that you do not need a writers' group, for a while or for good, and use other strategies, tactics and people to develop as a writer and to maintain your output.

A writers' group can go on indefinitely, as long as it proves purposeful, enjoyable and effective. After some time, you may find that it becomes something else – perhaps 'research group' would be a more appropriate term? – yet the term 'writers' group' has the strength of focusing on writing.

Once you are familiar with the processes of a writers' group, you may decide to set up a writers' group for postgraduates or researchers, so that they can focus on thesis writing and/or writing for publication.

Checklist for writers' groups

- Agree a common purpose: describe your writing projects to each other.
- Try working with a facilitator, at least for the first few meetings.
- Be flexible: adapt meeting times, agendas and formats to suit participants.
- Do some writing at each meeting – don't just talk about it.
- You could all be at different stages in writing – compare and contrast.
- Discuss barriers to finding writing time and develop solutions to them.
- Discuss writing-in-progress and work through 'clunky' stages of writing.
- Read each other's writing at different stages – give and receive feedback.
- Be prepared to debate each other's work.
- Relax and enjoy a stimulating exchange – be positive and constructive.
- Don't try to do all of these at every meeting!

- Agree a format for each meeting, but keep the talking-writing-talking sequence.
- Agree to review your experiences of the writers' group at a specified meeting.
- If it's not working, if you're not writing, move on.

Part III

In this final section, we set out our ideas about how you can include writing in a more integrated way into your life. Integrating writing into your life in ways that are satisfying and satisfactory is something that may require new habits and routines. We have already suggested how these habits and routines can be understood and initiated. These final chapters focus on how you can adopt a longer-term, even lifelong, approach to effective writing.

8

Redefining academic writing practices

Introduction • Redefining writing through teaching • Redefining writing through collaboration • Redefining writing through mentoring and networking • Redefining the competitive dimension of academic writing • Redefining the academy through healthy, functional writing dynamics • Checklist for an organizational approach to supporting writing

Introduction

All of the interventions outlined in Part 2 of this book have been designed in some way to help academics and academic developers to think about how they might go about writing differently and, in particular, more collaboratively than they might otherwise have considered. We have encouraged writers to think about using different mechanisms than are typically reflective of standard practice used in academic settings. In exploring the alternative routes to productive, effective academic writing we have highlighted that solitary, unsupported writing (while not the experience of all academics, some of whom have been involved in productive and supportive partnerships and groups from the very start of their careers) is a reality for many. It is this reality that makes writing at least occasionally feel fraught, grim and difficult.

This chapter makes explicit the features that we think should accompany the academic writing process in universities, features that might help us to think about ways in which we can work to redefine writing and, through that process, to make some positive steps towards redefining or reconceptualizing academia. We believe that by installing supportive principles of writing into academic environments, all members of the learning community stand to benefit. We do not ignore that academic writing has a strongly competitive dimension. But we also argue that if people adopt an exclusively competitive stance when writing in academia, they miss out on some of the most important benefits that can accrue by being part of a genuine learning community. Dysfunctional competition leads to a situation in which a few individuals benefit from academic writing, sometimes at the expense of many of their colleagues and students. Functional competition prevails in a situation where we have good role models, willing to share their expertise and to explore the journey from novice to expert for the benefit of everyone.

The competitive, individualistic paradox that prevails in many universities is one in which scholars are brought together under the same institution or disciplinary umbrella, and then somehow forced to work apart from and against one another. This dynamic has become increasingly problematic in educational institutions across the globe. Successful writers become more and more remote from the learning communities they are supposed to be serving, and a highly individualistic, competitive ethos prevails at the expense of community, teaching, learning, mentoring and developing. We have seen examples of settings where this is not the case, and believe that it is possible to create an alternative ethos – one that we explore in more detail in this chapter.

Redefining writing through teaching

Writing in university settings is a potentially powerful lever for teaching and for developing students' voices (Bean, 2001). The more aware an academic is about his or her own writing struggles, insecurities, strengths and achievements, then the more of a facilitator he or she can be in helping students to develop this skill in a self-aware, focused and effective way. Using freewriting exercises, helping people to become aware of what makes writing good or bad, according to whose rules and based on which criteria, encouraging students to reflect upon and to develop their ideas in writing, are all tools that can be used effectively in the classroom.

In particular, moving away from the idea that writing is simply the display of ideas, information and facts is an important shift (Elbow, 1973). Writing is an inherently creative process in which knowledge and ideas are not just shared or transmitted, but generated. It is through the process of writing that knowledge can be developed. Students in higher education environments often observe that in their learning experiences, they have few opportunities to test their own skills and to get feedback on how they are doing. This is especially the case in situations where resources are constrained and class sizes are large.

Empowering students to understand the benefits of constructive critique of one another's work creates a situation in which these resource constraints can genuinely be transcended, by inviting more active participation from students themselves and inviting them into the conversations, skills development arenas and debates that are potentially one of the most productive, creative activities associated with academia.

By getting students used to writing and by helping them to gain confidence in and familiarity with various forms of writing, including the rewriting dynamic that students so often dread, avoid or ignore, you may find that you have turned the key to the more 'self-directed' learning environments that higher and further education contexts are pursuing.

Some ideas for teaching through writing

Many of the readers of this book have probably already taught their students through writing. These suggestions may extend on or legitimize some of the teaching techniques that you already use. Whether this is the case, or the following suggestions are completely new to you, we have found that these simple approaches can create enriching and engaged learning environments, not just within a specific classroom but also beyond it. At the centre of these techniques is the idea that creating confident student writers is a natural extension to all of the benefits associated with creating confident faculty writers. It supports their learning, sets a stronger foundation for self-directed learning, encourages reflection and helps with the development, articulation and generation of ideas (Bean, 2001; Suchan, 2004). In addition, enhancing student writing strategies and processes is something that starts to improve communication and understanding between faculty and students in a way that transcends the problems that are often associated with 'different worlds in the same classroom' (Johnston, 2000). All of these benefits support sound pedagogy in a number of different ways and serve to create a community of practice in which the newest practitioners learn to sharpen and structure their thinking in ways that can help them to navigate academia more successfully.

1. Freewriting exercises

Freewriting is a technique that has been championed both by writers and teachers of writing for many years (see, for example, Elbow, 1981 and Murray, 2004). It is a technique that can develop more fluency and confidence among your students, can make writing a more routine habit in which they are more likely to be prepared to engage, and can provide insights both to teachers and students about each other's assumptions and ideas. A freewriting exercise can be very brief, embedded as a short slot within a standard lecture or tutorial, or it can form the central activity in any single teaching session. It can last anywhere from about five minutes to a couple of hours. The benefits of freewriting have been explored earlier in this book, but in particular, for students, it removes the responsibility that they often feel (and one that we have referred to frequently) for perfect, polished writing, and encourages them to produce text in whatever mode or sequence they choose. We have found that using freewriting makes students less self-conscious about how they express themselves, and more likely to focus on real ideas, questions and insights on which they can subsequently build.

Given that students learn effectively when they can link a new and unfamiliar topic to something that they already know, a useful freewriting exercise might be based on the following prompt: 'For the next 5 minutes, write down your thoughts on topic x [topic x can for example be the focus of your lecture, a topic they have expressed interest in or something that students have highlighted difficulties with]. This reflective writing can include anything that you think might be associated with the topic, anything you think you might already know about it, or anything that you think you might like to ask about its meaning or function.' What the prompt should do is encourage students to draw on their current frames of reference and knowledge bases before tackling the particular topic that you are going to teach them about. It provides them with momentum by demonstrating that even when not having been taught something, they are still likely to have questions, ideas and interesting attitudes about a topic. It can set the scene for their learning in a more motivated and focused way, and it can allow them to bring some of their own opinions and ideas to bear more deliberately on a learning session. All of this is more likely to create an active and engaged learning environment. It can be made more dynamic and more discursive by encouraging students to discuss what they have written in pairs or small groups before feeding back and proceeding with other aspects of the class.

Of course, you can choose your own prompts or encourage students to select from a range of writing prompt options. Whatever format you choose, if you urge students to write in their own words, not to edit while writing and to write in full sentences rather than short bullet points, what you are inviting them to do is to engage in their own proliferation of ideas and to articulate those at least initially to themselves. This is a skill and an orientation that applies writing directly to learning and helps students to develop a stronger sense of their own voice in advance of a formal learning session. This technique works well in many different kinds of learner contexts and can create active learning orientations even among very large groups of learners.

If your topic is something you think your students are likely to find very little to write about spontaneously, then take a few steps back – try to find something that you think will be closer to their frames of reference that might be a stepping stone to the ideas and concepts you are about to tackle in class. If you ask your students to write about something simpler or more accessible that is related to your topic, you will achieve two important pedagogical goals: firstly, it will help you to get closer to where they are, and secondly, it helps them to get closer to where you are. Asking them for permission to read their written reflections or to hear what it is they have written will further help you to get inside their heads and provide you with useful information that can help you to design your learning sessions with the benefit of the knowledge or orientations they have shared.

2. Generating criteria for good writing

Take a list of instructions for authors from a journal relevant to your discipline and ask students to 'translate' these instructions into a list of criteria that might help them to think about the features of writing they could install into their own work to make it more 'acceptable' or more 'effective'. Invite a debate about the difference between acceptability and effectiveness, and then have your students generate and negotiate an agreed list of 'features of good writing' that can act as a writing charter which can guide them in their efforts to write well, not just in your area of expertise but across all areas in which they are required to learn and write.

3. Mini critiques

Using the criteria that they may have developed themselves (see point 2 above), or criteria that you specify, ask students to review and critique each other's work. Guidelines for receiving and giving feedback that we have outlined in Chapter 3 could be useful in the implementation of this exercise.

4. Exploring rhetoric, argument, genre and grammar

Have students analyse different kinds of writing. For example, select abstracts or extracts from different disciplines that present ideas using different kinds of language, and ask students to explore these differences with a view to developing a greater understanding of issues of disciplinarity in writing (using the themes we explored in more detail in Chapter 4).

This exercise can be a useful and practical route to introducing students to philosophical ideas about knowledge (epistemology) and helping them to understand rhetorical differences or those associated with written debate and argument in different disciplines. Give students a simple lesson in good grammar. Have a debate about the importance of grammar. Explore the conventions associated with clear, accurate writing and encourage them to read the work of grammar enthusiasts (for example, Truss, 2003).

5. Reflecting through writing

Having students keep learning diaries, and reflect on their learning through writing, is another useful way in which teaching through writing can enhance learning experiences and environments. Students don't always see how far they have come at different stages in their learning journey. Written reflections can help them to trace their learning and to define key moments and stages of development (see, for example, Moore and Murphy, 2005). Alan Clark once famously noted that 'a day that goes unrecorded is a day that's disappeared' (quoted in Brandreth, 2006). Keeping a diary is a very effective way of capturing important insights and experiences, and doing these things relates probably most fundamentally to the reasons human beings started to write in the first place. Bringing this activity to your students as well as practising it yourself can reframe the writing process, making it meaningful and concrete and again feeding fluency and confidence in the activity it requires.

6. Student paper series

A powerful active learning context can be achieved by designing a student paper series system in a way that mimics the academic publishing process. It serves to educate students about how academic publishing works, and helps them to consider the issues of rigour, review and effective writing in academic settings. In order to launch a student paper series, you need to agree on a topic, or series of topics that your students should be prepared to write about, to take them through a set of criteria for effective written papers, to assign an editor and team of reviewers and to help them through the process of selection, review and feedback in a way that reflects the process of journal writing and publishing in academia. This exercise generally gives rise to rich and complex learning, not just about disciplinary content, but also about communication, the more subtle rules, routines and politics of writing, the articulation of arguments, the achievement of tasks according to scheduled deadlines and the giving and receiving of different kinds of feedback. It can also sustain learning by enabling both students and teachers to engage in a critical analysis of the politics of writing, something that can create another layer of insight and understanding among the students and teachers who participate.

Not only does this approach empower students to generate knowledge and to find effective ways of expressing it, but it also enhances faculty development too. One of the best ways to improve and enhance your own writing is to install creative ways of helping others to do so. Insights provided by students about the writing process, can be a wonderful reminder of some of the issues with which faculty themselves, albeit at another level, are struggling. Instead of viewing student writing as an 'add on' to their learning routines, writing is more usefully conducted as a central and integral part of learning processes and routines. The more you 'teach' writing within your discipline, the more of an expert you will become in defining and delivering on that task.

Redefining writing through collaboration

Learning is, and always has been, a social process. Learning theorists have, for a long time, highlighted the importance of interaction and collaboration when it comes to developing competence in particular tasks. This may be particularly true for the tasks associated with academic writing. Creating collaborative learning environments of the type described in Part 2 of this book, may be an important route to the positive redefinition of academic writing tasks, challenges and goals. Treating writing as a collaborative rather than isolated act is something that is a major theme of this book. Most importantly, this orientation helps to overcome the enormous divisions that exist in many academic lives. Academic activities tend to demand either high levels of extroversion (teaching, attending meetings, networking, presenting at conferences and so on) or high levels of introversion (e.g. independent reading, study and writing). Collaborating on writing projects is not just an important thing to do when different people have different skills to apply to a certain task (though it is also important for that reason), but behaviourally, it bridges the distance between introverted and extroverted type activities typical of many work contexts (Krebs Hirsh and Kummerow, 1996), often in very effective and potentially transformational ways. Collaborative writing does not mean producing text together, a process that Elbow and Belanoff (2000) point out is something that 'will drive you crazy' (p. 81). Rather, use collaboration as a way of generating ideas at the preparatory stage, of critiquing and building on the work produced by individuals in ways that can 'round out' the writing, and help individual writers to consider more fully issues of effectiveness, clarity, structure, evidence and so on. Simply put, collaborative writing is a way of broadening your base of writing support, of extending and substantiating your network and of making real the notion of 'communities of practice' in academic settings.

Redefining writing through mentoring and networking

Mentoring relationships are a significant key to career development. Across many careers, the existence of a mentor (or even more effectively, a network of mentors) has been shown to enhance a whole range of work-related factors such as job satisfaction, promotion chances, organizational commitment, role clarity, sense of identity and interpersonal skills (de Janasz, Sullivan and Whiting, 2003). The importance of mentors and networks in career development is even stronger for people in minority groups at work (e.g. Lankau & Scandura, 2002). General, research-based advice about mentoring and support networks could be usefully applied to our experience as writers in academia. Literature on mentoring suggested, for example, that mentoring and networking relationships give rise to positive results when those relationships are:

- Trust-based and 'power free', focusing on a genuine interest in mutual learning.
- Multi-source and multi-level – so that mentorees get advice from different people, with sometimes very different perspectives on issues and problems relating to their work (Ensher, Murphy and Sullivan, 2002).
- Monitored, nourished and adapted over time. Researchers have found that it is inadvisable to rely only on a single set of mentors as you encounter different problems and challenges (Vincent and Seymour, 1994). Different kinds of writing tasks, require different sets of mentors. Looking for synergies between people who can help you and vice versa may be an essential part of the pre-writing or incubation process.

Writing mentors are people who: listen to your ideas, read your work in progress, help you to develop your writing, encourage you when your energy or self-belief is flagging, criticize in order to enhance and sharpen your ideas, explore more possibilities than you might have considered on your own, expand on and develop ideas so that you can develop a writing strategy beyond any individual writing task, give feedback in the various ways that we have outlined in Chapter 3, ask questions that might not have occurred to you, remind you about possibilties or ideas that you have forgotten, and celebrate your writing successes.

Trust as an asset in the writing process

Trust is not only essential to emotional well-being, it also plays a central role in the development of good relationships among people at work. Nowhere is this more true than in academic environments. The literature on trust in organizations shows that high-trust groups are much more likely to create high-performance environments in almost all settings (Morley et al., 2004). And we, as writing developers, have certainly seen how groups of people who trust each other are more likely to create productive and mutually assisting writing patterns than those who don't. You can create conditions of trust by dismantling some of the barriers and boundaries that are often features of large bureaucracies. Simply by removing the normal structural barriers, even temporarily (as in writers' retreats and writing groups), you can build bridges between people and their disciplines that make it more likely they will work together to ensure better results for everyone than might be achieved when people work both alone and apart (Lee and Boud, 2003).

By giving people permission to admit their concerns about their own writing, you grant the same courage to larger groups of people and create an environment in which people help each other to overcome their blocks and weaknesses rather than concealing and fretting about them (Grant and Knowles, 2000). Academic environments characterized by mentors and writing networks will work better in pursuit of all academic goals than those without such supports.

Redefining the competitive dimension of academic writing

No matter how collaborative and shared our approaches to writing might become, it is simply not possible to ignore the fiercely competitive dimension of academic writing. As it is currently constructed, academic writing is indeed an inherently competitive process. We compete against others to get published, to have our ideas or findings heard, to legitimize our orientations among an increasingly international network of scholars and writers. More specifically, though, we compete with one another for the rewards associated with career progression and promotion. Sometimes this can make us feel like playing with our cards very close to our chests and cause us to feel that there are reasons to conceal and hide our work rather than share and discuss it with others. However, we believe that these instincts are becoming less and less relevant (if indeed they ever did serve a function). It is the increasingly global nature of academic competition that makes local support and help more relevant than ever before. As publishing and writing become more international, both giving support to and receiving it from our own colleagues in our own context makes more and more sense. There may come a time when you and a colleague compete for a single post or promotion that only one of you can get, but it is unlikely that your collaboration and mutual support will have damaged either of your chances – and it is indeed infinitely preferable than the tendency to conceal and withdraw from one another at a time when you need each other's help most. Despite the competitive terrain on which we all stand in the academic world, it is those academics who have developed trusting networks of supportive colleagues that derive the most pleasure and purpose from their working lives (see, for example, Anand, Glick and Manz, 2002). It is worth remembering this when you're considering the ideas and interventions that we have explored in Part II of this book.

As we said at the very beginning, what, how and for whom you write can have an enormous impact on your own individual career trajectory within academia. It is in recognizing that competitive reality that people often withdraw from dialogue with others about their writing goals and strategies. We advise you to do the opposite. A collaborative competition rises all boats whereas individualistic and sometimes dysfunctional competition creates unhealthy dynamics that undermine the spirit and purpose of education and of academia.

Redefining the academy through healthy, functional writing dynamics

Given that writing is usually a relevant and important work goal for almost all academics, the achievement of writing goals is likely to create healthier and more emotionally positive work dynamics (see for example Harris, Daniels and Briner, 2003). By creating supportive norms for academic writing, we can enhance the entire academy in focused and effective ways. The emotional challenges that people face when attempting to become confident, recognized, legitimate scholars in their field have started to be documented in literature on writing in general (see, for example, Holkeboer, 1986; Freidman, 1993) and on literature related to academic practice. Recognizing the emotional as well as the cognitive requirements of academic writing is central to the work both of individuals and their institutions, and in doing this, it may be possible to redefine universities and other higher education institutions in much more positive and synergistic ways. Writing is a concrete and demonstratable activity that can, if conducted effectively and with self-awareness, lead to improvements in teaching, research, collaborative learning and scholarly dialogue. It is in the interests of our students, our colleagues, our institutions and our societies that approaches to academic writing become more democratic, more accessible, more supported and more nourished. To put it in the words of Lee and Boud:

> The contemporary challenge for academic leaders is increasingly to bring academics into productive relationships with each other, to identify and support fundamental values and activities, including research.
>
> (Lee and Boud, 2003: 187)

Creating cultures that support positive and collaborative academic writing

Hofstede (1982, 1991) has shown how an organizational culture can be under-stood by examining heroes, rituals, symbols and values. We have seen how academic cultures can be changed and enhanced by a nurturing orientation to academic writing.

Heroes

Instead of just valorizing independent researchers who stay (or are kept) at a distance from students and novices, universities need to valorize those experts who are prepared to share their struggles with research and writing as much as they display their triumphs. Exploring the blocks, barriers, conundrums and learning obstacles that are part of everyone's writing experiences can help individuals and groups to make enormous leaps more quickly in academia. We need more reflective, and more humble, heroes – it is through this kind of leadership that new learners, students and novice writers develop the courage to use their own intellect in ambitious and creative ways. In addition, supporting people or mechanisms that act as facilitators of writing within academic environments will help to generate a more positive writing ethos among groups of academics.

Symbols

Such support can be sustained and reinforced through the use of symbols and signals within university and other higher educational settings. Signs on doors that say 'writers' group in progress', the cordoning off of writing corners and spaces in visible and well-resourced parts of the physical learning building start to transmit a message that writing is what we do, both apart and together; and such spaces, if well designed and welcoming, invite people to join in the process. If your institution wants to send a message that the writing process is important for learning, knowledge development and scholarship, it might also display pictures and symbols of great writers both creative and academic, provide faculty with essential writing tools or at least help to subsidize their purchase, and share interesting techniques and strategies that others have used. Organizational symbols are everywhere, and they have a powerful effect on the psyche of an institution. Writing environments are enriched if they incorporate writers in residence, scribes or writing facilitators who can help the academic community to translate good ideas into a rhetoric with which they may not yet be familiar. The existence of writing centres can also help both faculty and students to develop and enhance their writing. All of these (as well as providing substantial and practical help) will work symbolically to underline that the writing process is important and valued, nourished and championed. It is in valuing the process, as well as the product, that we can reap the benefits of writing for all areas of learning and scholarship.

Writing rituals

The rhythms and rituals of academic life are another way of creating, sustaining and reinforcing positive, collaborative writing routines. Traditionally, universities reward writing by examining someone's CV during selection and promotion decisions. While this might have rational wisdom on one level, it does little to create a shared understanding of the different writing journeys, successes, and achievements that colleagues have navigated. Positive writing rituals to create a greater shared understanding of what the process involves could include: writers' meetings for sharing, updating and developing work; regular writers' retreats like the one described in Chapter 5; writers' prizes administered regularly and with clear criteria for shortlisting and selecting winners; writing-related celebrations in which key achievements by either individuals or groups are endorsed and recognized.

All of these interventions (or even some of them) can enhance the values of academic practice in ways that get closer to the essence and purpose of higher education. By introducing, supporting and rewarding values that support writing through collaboration and dialogue, institutions communicate an important message: that sharing your writing activities and practices is important, that being and having mentors makes a difference, and that the process of writing is a positive, creative and celebrated one. We believe that these values can create much more positive and healthy writing dynamics in a whole range of academic environments.

Checklist for an organizational approach to supporting writing

Creating healthy and functional writing dynamics in higher education means creating organizational cultures that:

- Value, cherish and nourish the writing process as well as the writing output.
- Have a built-in organizational norm supporting the discussion and enhancement of early writing drafts (such as writing clinics, scheduled peer-supported interactions, as well as activities and rewards that value this norm).
- Have a built-in tolerance for writing 'failures' – recognizing that 'rejected' work can be building blocks for enhancing writing, not shameful testimonials of inadequacy.
- Subject the process of writing to analysis and reflection both for students and their teachers.
- Recognize that writing is something that can create, not just display, knowledge – thereby bridging the gap between the teaching and research functions within university and other higher education contexts (this idea will be developed further in Chapter 10).
- Recognize the competitive element of writing, but not at the expense of collaborative processes that have been proven to enhance overall writing norms and patterns among groups of academics.

9

Integrating writing into your life

Motivation to write • Behaviour change • An 'email trail' • Integrating your writing • Checklist

> If you don't have a programme, you have to invent a programme, and people should build that into their lives.

This quotation was provided by a writing mentor who had completed a university writing for publication programme and was reflecting on its implications both for himself, as a writer, and for other writers in the department. Whether there is, or was, or never has been a writing programme or writers' retreat in your department or institution, only you can genuinely build writing into your life.

This chapter describes a process that we argue is likely to support sustained writing activity over the long term. This process can increase the impact of other initiatives. Academics do not have to rely on a specific programme, but can develop what one writing mentor called a 'rolling process'. This is one way for you to put writing 'high on the agenda' in a way that is sustainable in the context of your own professional and personal life.

This chapter has relevance for those who have not participated in any type of writing programme. One approach is to develop a writing schedule: 'Scheduling helps us to integrate our writing much more effectively into the rest of our life' (Zerubavel, 1999: 5). Yet is the solution to the problem of integrating an activity into our lives as simple as 'scheduling' it?

- If it were simple, surely writing schedules would routinely be in place in departments?

- Surely academics know how to schedule their work, so as to make time for writing, as for any other activity?
- The principles of scheduling are, after all, relatively straightforward, yet academics acknowledge that creating a writing schedule and putting it into action are two separate, and difficult, processes.

What does not appear to be straightforward, among writers we talk to, is the change process required for academics to prioritize their writing. This suggests that the intention to write a specific piece or generally to publish more – and increased knowledge about how to go about it – may not be sufficient. Although intention is clearly an important factor, change must occur for that intention to be realized. Change, and more particularly how writers can sustain it, is the theme of this chapter.

Evidence for this may be found in academics' reports that development initiatives and schedules acted as a focus for further change. For example, the writing for publication programme led one academic to the realization that if he could manage his time differently, output would follow: 'Writing time is already there. I just have to manage it better.' He referred to changes he would have to make to his writing process. This typical example suggests that 'time' is not really the problem; changing how we use time is the challenge.

If you want to make time for writing, you may have to change, a complex process that requires analysis and reflection on other dimensions of your professional and personal contexts. Again, some academics wonder why this is not more straightforward. Perhaps it is because in writing programmes, where you advance your writing by practising certain strategies, the end of a programme comes as a transitional moment. This is when you start applying processes learned in one environment – a writing for publication pro-gramme, for example – in another context – your academic department, for example. The difficulty may lie in the fact that academics who 'retreated' from the context in which they were struggling to write in order to 'advance' their writing, then have to foreground, quite deliberately, processes they learned in the programme in the context of their professional and personal lives.

In the context of academic writing, a cognitive approach, such as providing information about planning and scheduling of writing, for example, will only take writers so far. For academics to change their writing practices requires modification on a number of levels. Integrating writing into your life requires you to review and adapt not just programmes and activities, but your values and beliefs about writing. We suggest that a sensible strategy is to take a tried and tested approach from another area – health promotion – and adapt it for academic writing. The strength of this process for managing change in health-related behaviour – such as taking up exercise or giving up smoking, for example – is that it engages all aspects of change: cognitive, behavioural and psychosocial. Having tried this approach with academic writers, we suggest that you use it to integrate writing into your life.

Motivation to write

In order to prepare to integrate writing into your life, you have to look at your motivation and weigh your motivation to write against your motivation to perform, and prioritize, other activities.

Balancing competing priorities, and the difficulty of protecting writing time, is a recurring issue in writers' discussions. If, as academics recognize, this is not simply a problem of 'time', but linked to factors that shape our motivation, then it is surely important that you consider these issues and develop a strategy for working on them. This will, of course, depend on your readiness to engage in a change process.

While your immediate aim may be, for example, to complete one piece of writing, the 'bigger picture' is about producing a range of written outputs over the long term. In addition, motivation may oscillate over the years, and you have to be skilled at managing the highs and lows of writing discussed in earlier chapters of this book.

The literature tells us that there are many ways to improve academic writing practices and outputs. However, if you are to learn about these well-established strategies and, in due course, adopt them, you must have, or develop, a strong motivation to write.

This may seem illogical; surely all academics are motivated to write for publication? However, the external rewards associated with academic writing are not automatic, results of writing efforts are not immediate and dedication to writing does not necessarily guarantee desired outcomes (such as publication, promotion or enhanced academic profile). This suggests that other 'bridges' between writing and its outputs may have to be understood, valued and constructed by the individual writer. The initiation and maintenance of productive writing behaviours may require other factors to be in place for the behaviour to become routine in your life.

In addition, research suggests that not all academics practise writing behaviours that are likely to lead to publication (Boice, 1987). Discovering and maintaining productive writing habits is not a straightforward process for all. Furthermore, research assessment exercises indicate that not all academics are able to publish to the same level. Even in pre-research assessment days, it is documented that productivity was limited to a few academics: 'Most papers are produced by few academic staff and . . . many faculty produce little or nothing' (Ramsden, 1994: 207).

The extent to which publication depends on writing skills alone – an argument that would, in any event, be difficult to sustain – is not the subject of this chapter. Instead, the focus is on those who want to write, are engaged in research, but recognize that they could improve their published output.

In addition, we suggest that it is timely to explore the important relationship between motivation and the use of effective writing strategies. This might begin to add to your understanding of how writing of the highest standard is produced, and information gathered could, in turn, be helpful in the development of novice researchers. For example, in some clinical subjects, it is important that best practice be communicated as quickly and as widely as possible, and that findings are tested in the peer review process.

It is not the purpose of this chapter to debate the questions of whether or not academics already have the prerequisite intellectual acuity, writing skills and quality of research to write about. Instead, the aim is to focus on behaviours that are likely to lead to writing for public output. This is not to say that acuity, skills and research are not important; rather, it is to explore the extent to which writing behaviours can help you to realize your potential in academic writing.

Behaviour change

There is a well-developed literature on behaviour change in the health professions, related to, for example, health promotion, where the aim is to enable people to adopt healthy behaviours in the interests of their own health. It is well known that such behaviour change, for example smoking cessation or exercise adoption, is complex and can be extremely difficult. However, health professionals have found that addressing the beliefs and values that underpin motivation is an effective way of helping people change their behaviours.

The aims of behaviour change in relation to academic writing may be defined as:

- To initiate and sustain beliefs and behaviours that support writing.
- To develop a strategy that you can sustain over the long term.
- To ensure that you have support for changes you make in your life.

The behaviour change process that has been adapted from the health professional context for academic writing consists of seven steps:

1 Assessing your readiness to change.
2 Using decisional balance.
3 Using a writing consultation.
4 Identifying barriers to writing and inventing strategies for overcoming them.
5 Setting realistic goals.
6 Relapse prevention.
7 Action planning.

It has been known for some considerable time that sustaining a specific behaviour requires more than existing or new knowledge of it (Bandura, 1977). In addition, behaviour change brings with it the risk of lapse or relapse to the original behaviour.

The model we have adapted focuses on a 'cycle' of change in relation to behaviour. It identifies the need for people to engage with the beliefs that underpin their behaviours and to access support and strategies to maintain their new behaviour. This, in turn, maintains and increases their confidence in their ability to change.

1. Assessing your readiness to change

We adapted the 'stages of change' model for academic writing. You can use this model to establish where you are in the change process. Think about where you are on the following scale. Which of these sounds most like you at this time? Assuming that since you are reading this book, you have an intention to write, you may find that the first two stages – 'pre-contemplation' and 'contemplation' – do not apply to you. Alternatively, there may be times when you know that you will not be able to write, and, for that period, you may place yourself at stage one, 'pre-contemplation'.

Stages of change

Pre-contemplation	'I have no intention of writing in the next 6 months'
Contemplation	'I am thinking about increasing my writing'
Preparation	'I do some writing, but not enough'
Action	'I have been writing, but only in the last 3–6 months'
Maintenance	'I have been regularly writing in the last 6–12 months'
	(Adapted from Marcus and Simkin, 1994)

It is likely that individual writers are at different stages of change. The aim here is not to think about developing one programme or schedule for all; nor is it a matter of finding one solution for all writers. This step is not simply about stating intention, but is the first step in the change process.

Those who stop at this point and promise themselves that they will act on their intention in ways that they have in the past, may or may not integrate writing into their lives. Moreover, an individual's sense of self-efficacy increases with each forward movement in a stage of change. For further changes to occur, other strategies will need to be in place.

Within this model people often move between stages, and it is normal for people to lapse and relapse from the different stages. For academic writers the aim is to move towards and stay in the 'maintenance' stage. This model provides the supportive framework to help you move in the desired direction of change, and to identify the times at which you are most likely to lapse or relapse into 'non-writing'.

2. Using decisional balance

Using decisional balance means comparing the perceived costs and benefits of writing. Once you have identified the stage of change that you are at, a decisional balance helps you to weigh up the pros and cons of writing, thus helping to reinforce the benefits and advantages of writing.

For this step, in two columns list the benefits to you of writing and the drawbacks, for you, of not writing. This step prompts you to explore the beliefs and values that underpin your behaviour in relation to academic writing. For example, here are the benefits and drawbacks identified by one academic writer.

Decisional balance

Benefits when you write	Drawbacks when you do not
Satisfaction	Feel like a failure
CV profile	Miss submission date
Get a paper in for conference	
May get a grant	

It may be more useful to make this balance of the pros and cons of academic writing the subject of peer discussion, and here again we can draw on an established model that is backed up by a well-developed literature, including a body of empirical research.

3. Using a writing consultation

Loughlan and Mutrie (1995) developed a one-to-one Motivational Consultation Process (MCP) as a procedure for promoting activity and exercise. This consultation uses a brief interview and negotiation to facilitate and support a person to change or maintain behaviour (Miller and Rollnick, 2002). There is evidence that this type of consultation has an impact on behaviour change (Hughes, Kirk and MacIntyre, 2002; Kirk, Mutrie and Fisher, 2004).

The relevance of the MCP to other contexts, and other behaviours, has been established. It was first adapted for use in the context of academic writing at the University of Limerick Writers' retreat in 2001 (Moore, 2003), where it was applied in the form of a 'writing consultation'.

For a writing consultation you work with a colleague who is prepared to act as consultant. The consultant's role is to help you to both identify issues and plan processes that are central to the success of your writing behaviour. The following are key features for the consultant aiming to develop an empathetic relationship with you for the writing consultation. (These could also be helpful for the general feedback sessions mentioned in Chapter 3.)

A writing consultation: the writing consultant's role

- Sit in a quiet place with your partner.
- Adopt an open body position.
- Keep good eye contact with your partner and actively listen to them.
- Attend, reflect back and paraphrase for the writer.
- Have an open, honest discussion.

You can probably think of colleagues who would be willing to work with you through this process and colleagues who would not. Having said that, you may get it wrong – you may find that your chosen peer, while effective in other modes, is not a suitable partner for this process. There may be lessons you can learn from this experience, but the main point is to keep looking until you find someone who is willing and able to adopt this process and work with you as you go through it. It has to be emphasized that the literature on this approach advocates working in a one-to-one set-up. Persevere until you make it work for you.

When we first tried the writing consultation with academic writers, one intriguing outcome was participants' identification of the benefits of *not* writing, a feature that was not included in the existing model:

Benefits of not writing

- Not having to test yourself.
- Not having to 'face your demons'.
- Not subjecting yourself to criticism.
- Not facing 'things' you don't want to face.
- Avoiding the struggle of making time to write.
- Not having to deal with colleagues' reactions to your writing.

Whether or not it is useful to include this subject, as part of writers' behaviour change process is not yet clear, but it did resonate for academics participating in this initial trial of the process, does identify barriers to academic writing and is related to writers' values and beliefs.

One academic who read about our approach asked whether there were any pitfalls to watch out for. The most obvious, and perhaps likely, is writers fixating on problems and barriers, rather than negotiating strategies for overcoming them. We have heard of writers' meetings where this happened. The writing consultation is designed to move writers beyond this fixation, prompting you to review your values as a first step in the change process.

The next step is to work through the following sections with your colleague still acting as a writing consultant.

4. Identifying barriers and inventing strategies for overcoming them

This is a key step in the negotiation of writing into your life: identifying barriers to your writing and finding ways to overcome them. This may take time. Your writing consultant may have to be patient or persistent or both, prompting you to think of new strategies.

List barriers to writing and strategies for overcoming them. Here is one academic writer's example:

Barriers	Strategies
Fear	Talk and compare experiences with trusted others
Writing block	Use your 5-minute writing and prompts
Poor reviews	Analyse, deconstruct and devise a positive response

Again, the emphasis is on overcoming barriers to change. These should be related to your values and beliefs, which you identified in a previous step.

5. Setting realistic goals

The next step is to set short- and long-term goals that are realistic and time bound. Academics often know only too well what their writing goals are, but frequently we find that these goals are not very specific. In many cases writing sub-goals are not defined at all.

What we do know is that in the absence of a specific goal for writing it is difficult to use what little time there is usefully. Even when time is used for writing, you may sometimes be left feeling discontented with your output or text because there is no way to measure the extent to which you have progressed towards the ultimate goal. Over time, this can be demoralizing, and can undermine your intention to write. That is why this step is so important.

Still working with your writing consultant, list your long- and short-term goals:

- What is/are your long-term writing goal(s)? . . .
- What is/are your next realistic short-term writing goal(s)? . . .

6. Relapse prevention

However, even well-defined goals do not ensure that new behaviours are immediately adopted. Relapse is part of the change process. In the context of academic writing, 'relapse' means reverting to old writing behaviours and abandoning new behaviours that support writing.

This is a key innovation in the adapted behaviour change model described in this chapter: anticipating relapse situations for the stage of writing you are in, and identifying strategies for preventing relapse. This is a crucial part of change process; you not only anticipate where your new behaviour is likely to fail, but also plan a strategy to prevent that happening.

- What high-risk relapse situation(s) will stop you achieving your writing goal?
- What are your likely relapse situations?
- When are you likely to give up your writing time?
- Which tasks do you have coming up that are likely to interfere with your plans?
- How will you prevent this?

Work through these questions with your writing consultant. Discuss what you can do to avoid relapsing to your old behaviours and maintain your new behaviours.

Here is one example from the group that tried the writing consultation for the first time at the Limerick University writers' retreat:

Relapse	Strategy
Teaching in semester 1	Monday: give students directed reading (3 hrs)
Mother not well	Get brother to look after (2 nights/week)
Marking	Mark five papers, then break and write

Note how specific these strategies are. These participants invented new strategies, indicating that the process of change had begun. The strategies were new to these writers – they had not considered them before.

7. Action planning

The final step is creating an action plan, including meeting for review, support and encouragement. These are necessary to sustain your change process. Take each of your writing goals, both long and short term, and plan your actions for achieving them.

- Actions you will take in order to achieve long-term goals . . .
- Actions you will take in order to achieve short-term goals . . .

Those who have most experience of working with people using this model – those working in the health professions, for example – tell us that people using this change process for the first time often confuse 'actions' and 'goals'. It is therefore worth clarifying that in this context 'goals' are what you want to achieve in your writing, while 'actions' are the step(s) you will take in order to achieve them.

If you find that your goals and actions overlap, it may be because you have not defined your intended actions. Your writing consultant may spot this, but, if they lack experience in using this model, they might not. It is probably a good idea to discuss this goals/actions distinction with them.

Once you have discussed and noted your planned actions, set a date and place for your next meeting with your writing consultant. This step is important because the model is more likely to work if you have a system of reviewing and recording your achievements. Without that, you may lose focus on your progress.

An 'email trail'

One way of tracking your performance and progress towards your goals is to use an email trail. This is one way of monitoring your actions, using the change process described above, over a period of time. Constructing an email trail of your writing means, firstly, deciding that you have reached a point where you need to analyse your writing activity in order to change it and/or consolidate the change process by monitoring it more closely. You may also want to get a better picture of your writing process. In other words, it comes back to your motivation not just to write, but to learn how to improve your writing.

Once you have decided to try this, your next step is finding someone who will receive your regular emails, perhaps once a week, in which you will report on your progress with your writing project. The specific content of your emails is up to you, except for the stipulation that you write about your writing. Your time commitment is, on average, ten minutes per week, producing emails of around two hundred words each. The recipient of your emails can decide how much time to allocate to reading and responding to them, and you can agree this before you start.

The email trail will heighten your awareness of the integration process within the context of your actual writing life. This is distinct from monitoring, or concordancing, your writing by analysing discourse features (Coniam, 2004). While concordancing involves analysing your writing in terms of the sentence structures you use, for example, an email trail involves analysing your writing behaviours, attitudes and outputs.

This may mean writing about your intentions to write or theorizing about writing, but it must include, for at least some of the time, describing your writing activities, expressing your feelings about your writing and monitoring your progress in terms that seem appropriate to you. The recipient of your emails does not have to reply to them all, although you may occasionally ask for a response, just to reassure yourself that someone is attending to what you say. There is no onus on the recipient to help you to solve your writing problems or provide feedback of any kind, since that might begin to shape the content of your emails. The purpose is to create a virtual space where you can reflect freely, in your own words, on your actual writing practices.

Over time, in the course of a year, for example, your emails will reveal aspects of your writing practice that you had not noticed before. Taken together, your emails can show you where events and patterns affect your productivity. They create a body of information about your writing that you can analyse, with some distance and perhaps less subjectivity.

Purposes of an email trail

- Articulating the highs and lows of academic writing.
- Defining the real-time dynamics of the writing process.
- Revealing relationships between writing and other tasks and actions.
- Unpacking iterations in the writing process.

Your emails may show you that you have a writing crisis each time you have a set of papers to mark, or a health crisis every time you present at a conference in December, or dips in your output or motivation when you try to write at these times. Some of this you might have noticed already, but your noticing might not have triggered any action. You may have to decipher the precise combination of factors that led to these effects, since it is not the writing itself that is the cause. It is your approach to it. Your emails can also reveal the factors and conditions that allow you to write productively.

Deciphering these patterns can prompt you to change your writing habits, set more realistic goals and give yourself permission not to write at certain times. This in turn can improve both your motivation to write and your ability to act on that motivation.

At the very least, writing these emails constitutes writing practice, but looking at your emails as an email trail is to engage in a dialogue, as much with your writing self as with the person who agreed to receive your emails. The email trail prompts you to reflect on the specifics of your practice, your motivations and patterns in your personal and professional lives. It creates a virtual space where you can 'act out different attitudes and values' (Boud and Walker, 1998: 199). It allows you to compare your writing practices with those of experienced writers (Hartley and Branthwaite, 1989).

The email trail is another way in which academic writers can invent a form of regular dialogue about writing, if that is not available in another form, and we know that in many academic contexts it is not. In practice, in academic settings, there is little of this in-depth reflection on process. Nor is there generally a forum for expressing what might be multiple subjectivities related to writing.

To illustrate, here are extracts from one writer's email trail, written over a period of 16 months:

> I suppose the greatest obstacle to writing at work is my own attitude. I have a real problem in convincing myself that the writing is part of what I am employed to do. I regard it as something that is for my own benefit and feel a bit guilty about being paid to do it [5 April] . . . There are many obstacles to the writing process . . . priorities of work and home life, inappropriate conditions for writing and the inability to get started . . . there is lack of confidence that the paper will be of a sufficiently high standard to withstand scrutiny by experts [18 May] . . . I had been putting off sending you a message because I had achieved so little this week [15 December].

This writer also sent an email, at another point in the academic year, which was only one line long: 'These exam papers are driving me mad'. Much later, when he looked back over his collection of emails written during a year, he was able to reflect on his earlier practices, consolidate perceived changes in disposition towards writing and identify aspects of his writing that presented persistent challenges.

This email trail showed that specific writing strategies had proved successful for this writer during this period. In addition, there was an acceptance of certain constraints, which had not been there at the start, and he had adopted a problem-solving approach:

> I have to accept that [marking] will eat into time set aside for writing, and I will therefore have to try to find an equal amount of time at work for research to compensate.

This is not to say that he had solved all his writing 'problems', nor do these emails constitute 'evidence' of productivity, nor can the email trail be taken as a comprehensive record of performance or practice. What the email trail does is shed light on writing practices.

Some will argue, again, that this is no substitute for 'just writing', but, again, the counter-argument must be that not everyone manages that. For some academics, writing is not as simple as just sitting down and getting on with it, and we know that even those who have excellent writing skills may still have problems finding time to write. Given the insights that an email trail can provide, it is a good investment of your time. You can scrutinize your values, beliefs and practices using an email trail. It might otherwise be difficult to see these as clearly.

You may begin, for example, to see what forms the necessary iterations – that are so much the subject of this book – look like in the context of your own practice. This is not to say that these will be constants, in any sense, but you can establish the range of processes you use and assess your use of them. You can also monitor your reactions to iteration itself. It may be that only once you have begun to reflect on iterations in your writing process do you see that while iteration sometimes seems to be a point of retreat, it is often a point of advance in a writing project. With this in mind you can begin actively to manage such iterations, secure in the knowledge that they are a sensible, workable and effective dimension of your writing process. If, on the other hand, you judge that they are not effective, then you can adapt them.

Similarly, you may be able to track the 'advance-retreat' dynamic, and this in turn may help you to set more realistic goals and to manage your writing time better. These ideas are likely to remain abstractions until you can relate your own writing experiences to them. This may be where much of the 'problem' of writing lies: the writing 'product' – the publication – has so much value attached to it, while the writing process has so little relative value that it routinely receives much less attention. Without such reflection, it is difficult to modify the process with any confidence. This is why it is so important, as was explained in the previous section, to anticipate relapse situations and, if they still occur, to reflect on the strategies you have been using. The email trail can help you do this.

The strategies we propose throughout this book will take time to 'bed in', and the email trail will allow you to track your developing writing process. This can be an effective device for monitoring your adoption of new strategies, allowing you to review, reshape and retune. Perhaps more importantly, it can help you to ask 'why' certain strategies work and others fail, for you. The 'why?' question is often the missing link in our reflections on writing.

Above all, there is value, potentially on several levels, in regularly writing to someone who sees you are a writer. Perhaps more importantly, there is value in positioning yourself as a writer, and then, looking back at your collection of emails, to see yourself as the type of academic writer who is managing the advance-retreat dynamic.

Integrating your writing

Having explored the psychological processes that can help you integrate writing into your life, we now provide a concrete example of integration. Writing a book is one way of integrating your writing, in the sense that it allows you to bring your ideas – and perhaps your published papers – together. Gordon (2004) represents publishing as a form of 'cross-promoting':

> Remember that if you intend to make professional publishing an integral part of your . . . career, you are unlikely to stop with one book or article. Cross-promote your own work; draw upon and cite your previous writing. . . . Just as all professional communication is mutually reinforcing, so too do your professional activities and your writing work together in building your career and promoting your work – and yourself!
> (Gordon, 2004: 113)

Integrating writing into your life may involve creating internal integration in your body of work. It is unlikely, and probably unwise, to aspire to tackling a completely new subject in every paper. Instead, you can plot several connected papers.

While writing a book may seem, to those who have never done it before, to be a monumental undertaking – and in some research assessment exercises a book may 'count' for less than a paper – it can prompt you to find ways to write regularly. Perhaps even more than when you are writing journal articles, when you are writing a book you have to invent writing processes that fit into your life. Since, in some disciplines, and for some publishers, writing a book lets you write more in your own voice and about your own views than is possible for journal articles, this may be more motivating. Your book may be more closely aligned with your values and beliefs, and, as we know from the literature on behaviour change referenced above, this can support your intention to become a regular writer.

Writing a book is represented below as a process, so that these steps can be scheduled into real time.

From idea to book: a process

- Review publishers' and colleagues' websites.
- Find commissioning editor(s): name(s) and email address(es).
- Email: an 'initial inquiry'.
- Complete publisher's proposal form (read guidance notes).
- Discuss your questions with commissioning editor(s), e.g. book length.
- Submit proposal, chapter outline and other material.
- Check that it arrived.
- Your proposal goes out to reviewers.
- Check date for feedback from reviewers ('date for your diary').
- Reviews come back – revise proposal.
- Contract signed.
- Use publisher's style guide.

- Write manuscript, submit by deadline.
- Ask for extensions well in advance.
- Check copy-edited typescript.
- Check proofs.
- Write index (or pay to have it done for you).
- Complete publisher's author questionnaire (may be earlier).
- Write blurb for the back of your book.
- Check publication date.
- Plan a book launch – send out invites.
- Send copies/flyers to colleagues.
- Attend a conference where your publisher has a display.

You can engage in informal dialogue with publishers as you develop your publication plans, at almost any stage in the book writing process. If you decide to write a book proposal, you will, of course, use the publisher's form, but a generic template, including most of the key headings, is provided in Murray (2006).

The processes described in this chapter may constitute the necessary negotiations for developing your writing strategy to the extent that you not only write more, but also integrate writing into your life. Research suggests that these steps will help you achieve this, so that writing remains on your agenda, along with all your other activities:

On-going discussion of writing waned when the programme finished, except for one or two people. It's not as high on the agenda. It's like everything else: when the programme stops the focus is lost. Research has become more closeted.

(Writing mentor in a university writing for publication programme)

This quotation defines a recurring problem that is addressed in this chapter: while initiatives described in previous chapters are effective, in terms of positive impact on academic writers' output and processes, when the programmes end, some academic writers say that they lose momentum, as writing gives way to other activities, and the culture for writing 'wanes'.

This effect may indicate the limited impact of such programmes, although participants report that they help them to get their writing under way and, in many cases, to become regular writers. Alternatively, it may take us back to the starting point of this chapter: only the individual writer can build writing into his or her life. In small-scale studies, using follow-up interviews designed to explore individual's processes, attitudes and negotiations, it emerged that those who continue to write had found 'places' for writing:

Where is writing?

- In formal and informal development activities.
- In peer relationships.
- In the academic's professional life.
- In classroom activities.

Integrating writing into your life may also mean finding times when you do not write, if your email trail, or other process, reveals that there are specific, recurring time slots when you know that your writing gives way to other activities. If writing is integrated into your life you can do this in the knowledge that, in due course, other activities will, in their turn, give way to writing.

For this to occur, for some academics, there is a need for sustained negotiation between different academic roles, and negotiation between the two main academic roles – teaching and research – is addressed in the next chapter.

Checklist

- Decide whether or not you want to fit writing into your life.
- Assess how important writing is to you.
- Integrating writing in your life may mean changing your writing behaviours.
- Behaviour change can be managed as a process.
- Start by articulating your beliefs and values, in relation to academic writing.
- New knowledge about writing is unlikely to produce behaviour change.
- Document your actual writing practices in some form, e.g. an email trail.
- Integrate your writing by making connections between your writings.
- Clarify the distinction between your writing goals, plans and actions.

10

Using writing to reconcile teaching–research tensions

Academic writers' experiences of the teaching–research tension •
Teaching–research synergies • Checklist

While the previous chapter dealt with strategies for integrating writing into your life, this chapter focuses on one potential barrier to writing in more depth. Academics tell us that a major barrier to research is teaching; teaching and research seem, for some at a certain point in their careers, for others more permanently, to be in constant tension, and this often places planned writing time in direct opposition to the teaching timetable.

Some academics find that this tension stops them from doing any research at all, while others find ways to resolve the tension. Even academics who have published before, who have the requisite research skills and a body of material to write about report that creating time for research is a constant process of negotiation. Few academics report that they have never perceived a tension between teaching and research.

The idea of a teaching–research tension may have its origins in a perception of the two activities as being fundamentally different. For some, the distance between the two activities seems impossible to bridge. In addition, there is a perception that teaching and research do not have the same value in academic life, that research is assumed to have more value than teaching. At the same time, teaching has priority. This can create huge tensions.

Some academics feel that there simply is no time for research, no room to manoeuvre and no way to negotiate change, and some do indeed have too heavy a teaching load. This position may relate to the type of contract on which they are employed. It is not our purpose in this chapter to minimize this problem, but we do want to encourage academics in this position not to see themselves as the 'sacrificial lambs', 'dogsbodies' or 'teaching drones' of the system. We have heard such terms used. We have heard accounts of academics who feel that, on days when many or all of their colleagues are away from the department – doing research, writing or external work – they feel that they have to 'be there' for the students, since no one else is available to deal with students' inquiries and problems. This cuts into their research time.

Being positioned in this way is a key mechanism of the teaching–research tension, particularly, but not exclusively, for younger, newer staff. New academics tell us that they are often allocated first-year classes, leaving them not only little time for research, but also no opportunity to make connections between their teaching and their research and no hope of developing an area of expertise.

However, while some academics portray teaching as the enemy of research, others point to synergies between the two. Some maintain that there are direct links: good teachers are in touch with, if not active in, research, and good teaching is informed by research. In practice, such synergies between teaching and research may be more complex than some would have us believe. In this chapter we argue that, rather than adding to the teaching–research tension, writing is one way of resolving it. Teaching, regularly defined as a barrier, can be used as a lever.

If you want to write, it seems inevitable that you will have to develop strategies for navigating the teaching–research tension. Even when you feel that your teaching workload leaves you no time for writing, you still have options. You can develop a strategy for dealing with these tensions, so that when there are those 'magic moments', when teaching–research synergies emerge, you know that while the teaching–research tension may resurface, you have ways to resolve it. This may be through teaching–research synergies, such as those described in this chapter (see also Chapters 6 and 7).

The purpose of this chapter is to help you develop approaches for integrating teaching and research through your writing. This introduction has explained why we focus on the teaching–research tension: because it is so frequently invoked by academics who struggle to make time – or as much time as they would like – for their writing.

The next section analyses academics' experiences of the teaching–research tension in order to shed light on the underlying factors, a key factor being the tension between perceived institutional values and personal values. While there are many ways in which perceived institutional values differ from personal values, across institutions, the gap appears to be particularly acutely felt at the teaching–research nexus.

The final section describes coping strategies: potential teaching–research synergies that can help you to resolve the teaching–research tension through writing about teaching.

Academic writers' experiences of the teaching–research tension

The teaching role has changed in recent years: in addition to putting in an agreed number of teaching hours, academics are required to be competent, perhaps more than competent, in teaching. Beyond initial qualification in teaching and learning in higher education, there are other activities to provide continuous professional development. This all takes up more time and, potentially, increases the pressure on research time.

It may be that the balance is shifting, in terms of the traditional differences between teaching and research, now that the value of a scholarly approach to teaching is more widely understood. Alternatively, you may feel that teaching and research remain radically different activities:

> Traditionally it has been assumed that there is a clear distinction between the worlds of research and the worlds of policy and practice – that there are 'two communities'. On the one hand there is the world of research, based on explicit, systematic work aimed at the growth of theoretical knowledge. Practice and policy on the other hand are seen as taking place in the 'real world', a world based on different forms of knowledge – for example on tacit knowledge and on practical wisdom.
>
> (Furlong and Oancea, 2005: 5)

While this quotation identifies the polarization of research, on the one hand, and policy and practice, on the other, the paper from which it is extracted made the case for new definitions of research. In doing so, it raised some of the issues that may lie at the heart of the teaching–research tension. Teaching and research have for some time seemed to constitute 'two communities', each with its own values, priorities and discourse. Perhaps it is time to analyse this sense of difference in order to explore the source of the tension.

The teaching–research tension

- Is it about lack of time?
- Is it caused by overload in teaching duties?
- Is tension caused by differences in philosophy or conceptions of 'research'?
- Are there 'two communities', with academics forced to take sides?

- Has research in some disciplines lost touch with the 'real world'?
- Has that not changed in the past ten or twenty years in many disciplines?
- Is there still a hierarchy: research over teaching?
- Is that what undermines academics' motivation to write for academic journals?

Since a perceived teaching–research tension is repeatedly identified by academics as a barrier to writing, we explored this tension in some depth by interviewing a selection of academics. We wanted to find out what forms the teaching–research tension takes, how it interacts with other factors and issues and whether or not is was possible to define it further. Above all, we wanted to explore academics' perspectives on teaching–research tensions.

What we found is that the balancing act is complex; managing the teaching–research tension was not, for the academics we interviewed, simply a matter of improving time management skills – a recurring response to academics' complaints that there is no time for research.

We regularly interview academics who participate in writers' groups or programmes, in order to develop our understanding of their experiences and of successful and unsuccessful practices. For example, we often follow emerging narratives of their writing lives, using one-to-one interviews of about an hour.

Our intention is not to evaluate either writers' outputs or the long-term impact of the writers' group they attended. Instead, we want to find out what they think about research and writing, what is on their agendas, not ours. We aim to 'activate narrative production' by academics (Ritchie and Rigano, 2001: 755). Any 'themes' that emerge from these interviews are introduced and developed by the academics themselves.

Although it was not our intention to put teaching–research tensions on the agenda of these conversations, interestingly teaching–research tensions were raised by most interviewees, in relation to their own research. A selection of recurring comments relating to teaching–research tensions are dealt with here.

While we recognize that the academics with whom we had these discussions were a self-selecting group, and while we did not attempt to adjust for bias, we consider that we can, nevertheless, present their insights here, at least as starting points for our – and your – exploration of teaching–research tensions.

The small minority of academics who do not mention teaching–research tension during such discussions tend to discuss previous, current and ongoing projects, suggesting that they are writing regularly and have resolved the tension in some way. A slightly larger minority raise the teaching–research tension only to dismiss it; it is not, for them, a barrier to research or writing. They recognize that it is an issue for others, but not for them. The majority of academics, unprompted, identify teaching–research tensions, and these seem to be of three types:

1 The teaching 'buzz'.
2 The teaching imperative.
3 The theory–practice divide.

1. The teaching 'buzz'

> I can be as high as a kite, getting the students laughing one minute or going all quiet when I was reading them something today . . . thinking to myself, 'I'm really performing here'. Research doesn't give me that to the same extent.

For some academics, the teaching–research tension is expressed in terms of the different levels of satisfaction that come with each activity: research is sometimes not a priority for them because teaching is more motivating and more rewarding. Academics may be confident in the teaching role, but less so about research or about writing to a standard acceptable for academic journals. Teaching provides an immediate response; with research, you might not know for months or years how your work is received.

The teaching–research tension is often identified, without any prompting on the subject, as a current issue in academic departments, affecting, for example, how 'an hour' of work is defined, with colleagues debating the relative difficulty of teaching at different levels, or comparing the level of 'difficulty' in teaching with that of 'sitting writing and thinking for an hour'. In some contexts, certain activities are perceived to be more highly valued than others: 'It even comes down to courses – teaching on certain courses has more status than teaching on other courses.' This can be divisive: 'It's forcing folk to almost take sides'. However, many academics acknowledge this as a feature of their working life generally, rather than of teaching and research exclusively: 'The hierarchies are there with other issues.'

The relative value attached to teaching and research can also affect the perception and self-perception of academics performing these roles, and, since we know that self-perception and values are central to an academic's motivation, this may influence their decisions about how – or whether – to make time for research.

Most academics seem to be aware that it is the individual's responsibility to navigate a way in this culture – 'There is an element of put up and shut up' –, acknowledge that they do have 'choices' in how their time is allocated to different duties, and could make a case for more research time. Apparent ambivalence towards this 'choice' could be taken as an indication of unwillingness to do research, or it may show a lack of understanding of what it involves. Yet, even academics who have experience of and insight into research and academic writing still experienced these problems.

2. The teaching imperative

Writing and research time were promised, but it's always the first to go.

Even though I have acknowledged writing time, it is seen as flexible time. You can still be given teaching. The principle of having a block of time is applied, but it's not treated as sacrosanct, which is how it should be.

Research is regarded by many academics as an 'at risk' activity, in the sense that workload allocations do not seem – or do not seem to them – to include research time. In one department a strategy for allocating time – a writers' group – had been formally agreed, but had never been put into action.

In this perceived context, negative responses to their work seems to have an even more damaging and demotivating effect on some academics, and the perception of the culture in one department – 'everyone is busy on their own things' – could be interpreted as a need for support and/or validation. Some academics seem to lose the ability to intervene, once this process has started: 'I allowed my job to swamp me, particularly the teaching side.' This academic did not attribute this problem to the teaching–research tension specifically, nor did he or she attribute it to other external factors. The point was that, in hindsight, this academic could see that the teaching–research tension was a fact of life.

While they acknowledge their responsibility to organize their time, academics often find that even if teaching comes second to research in some sense, teaching holds a 'premium' when it comes to scheduling. This differential valuation is perhaps at the heart of teaching–research tensions, and might explain academics' apparent self-contradictions, as they frequently appear to shift their evaluation of the two activities. This reveals what they see as the operationally contradictory requirements of teaching and research.

In addition, teaching is perceived, in some contexts, as having a 'premium' that research does not: 'The new workload . . . new masters course . . . developing new modules . . . This is the driver at the moment. You have classes sitting in front of you to get on with.' This seems to be a widespread problem: when you have been allocated a certain number of teaching hours, and you know that students are going to be sitting in front of you, you have no flexibility. There is no way of finding 'extra' time for research. The 'teaching imperative' is accentuated by the funding mechanism: if you do not teach, you have no income, and if you do not diversify your provision – by developing new masters courses, for example – you lose your share of the market. It is in these terms, academics tell us, that teaching is positioned as the 'driver' in a way that research is not.

The imperative to develop new courses comes up frequently in our discussions with academics. As new courses are launched there are, usually, significant increases in teaching load, with no real compensation in terms of research time. Many departments do not appear, according to these accounts, to balance teaching and research. As before, academics acknowledge that they are notionally in charge of their own time, but some seem to lose, or give up, control as new courses are developed and make new demands on their time. The lack of accountability for research, compared to teaching, is a problem. Research assessment exercises only monitor outputs every few years.

What emerges from our discussions with academics is that they know that they are expected 'just to get on with' research, and yet they can still find themselves unable to progress. We can speculate that this may result from their internalizing the devaluation of research. If this seems to be a misrepresentation of mature academics as overly passive, as if they were colluding in the marginalization of their research, then we can only remind you, if it needs to be said, that the influence of departmental cultures can be powerful. The words, 'Pull yourself together' or 'Just start writing' have been said to academics who raise these issues, and, while these might be well intentioned, they miss the point – that it is easier said than done. Besides, many academics, in spite of heavy teaching and administrative loads, do successfully complete research projects, but still face problems.

The expectation that academics will conduct research is based on the assumption that they know how to, and those who do not know feel that they are falling short and lose confidence either to try or to ask for support. The broader problem lies in lack of research training – in some disciplines – as much as in the teaching–research tension.

This analysis reinforces points made in earlier chapters of this book: that making time for research, and for writing, is not the problem. Establishing that these activities have value to the individual academic is the first step. If that personal value is undermined by external factors, other forms of support may be beneficial. This lends further weight to the argument for writers' groups to support even some relatively experienced academic writers.

3. The theory–practice divide

> Our ability to influence practice is less. We produce all this writing for journals to feed the RAE [Research Assessment Exercise] need, and [professionals] become increasingly hostile at what they see as empty theory.

This is a real issue for academics in some disciplines, and less so in others. For some academics in the discipline of Education, for example, this issue has prevented them from identifying the purpose and benefit of doing research. For them, working with, and writing for, practitioners has much more value. In Education this is how they improve teaching:

> I'm very proud of these [publications] because they tie up a lot of the ideas I'm interested in and will affect practice, and I had to overcome writing barriers to do them.

Similarly, in the health professions, you improve patient care by developing practice. The extent to which this view is characteristic of those who are new to research is not clear. What is clear, however, is that there are potential teaching–research tensions in the perceived meaning of research and writing for academic journals.

For some academics this is an explicit choice, a strategic decision aligned with their own values. However, even having made this choice, they still voice concerns, doubts and admit to low self-esteem, related to the low status of teaching in relation to research in their institutions: 'I feel I'm not as well regarded because I don't write and publish.' These academics, in discussion, seem to oscillate between pride in their work, one moment, and writing it off, the next. The teaching–research tension seems to be a matter of the gap between some academics' values and perceived institutional, or peer, values related to research and certain types of writing. This is not to claim insight that these academics do not have themselves, since they are able to see contradictions in their analyses: 'is that overstated? I'm not comfortable with that view.' Perhaps their apparent ambivalence is about shifting positioning during these discussions: from 'proud' published researchers to 'insecure' non-researchers.

Ironically, for some academics working in the discipline of Education, the research–teaching tension becomes a deterrent to researching and writing about it for practitioners. Yet, most of these academics continue to write for different purposes, and many hold research grants. In other words, it is not that they reject research; instead, they identify the tension as not of their making, while acknowledging their responsibility for dealing with it.

However, these are accomplished, thoughtful, motivated and self-aware people. They know the potential consequences of not doing research for their careers in higher education. We can speculate that the teaching–research tension persists for some if they are still in transition to higher education, and still adjusting their values and practices to this context.

We should not ignore the fact that many academics find that the teaching–research tension is acute. This seems to be particularly the case for academics appointed to full-time jobs while studying part-time for a doctorate. Some institutions allocate research time, in some cases a day per week, but others do not. On top of this, the academic who is also a doctoral student has to find some way to publish in journals and may, at the same time, be taking a course on teaching and learning in higher education.

Academics who are committed teachers are often put off research by its perceived nepotism, and are dismayed at what appears, to them, to be the erosion of academic values: 'There's a dirtiness to the whole thing. . . . It's who knows who.' However, academics who put this view, in such terms, are generally aware of the danger of overpersonalizing the issue, of becoming, as one put it, 'too self-interested in research'. Once again, therefore, the teaching–research tension is not, in itself, the problem; the academic's values, and perception of values held by published writers and editors, are also barriers.

What emerges from our reflections on what academics say about the teaching–research tension is that teaching is not the enemy of research; it is the conflict between perceived institutional values and individual values that is the problem. In addition, there is perceived conflict between the value institutions purport to attach to research and the allocation of time for research.

What is striking about academics' accounts of teaching–research tensions is that all of them take responsibility for their writing barriers, in the sense that they recognize, cognitively, that only they can change things. However, this realization is not always sufficient to change habits or approaches. They can only change what they have control over, and many feel that they have no control over their teaching workload.

These accounts will be seen by some as nothing more than 'excuses', but we have chosen to devote some time to unpacking these positions. In the current higher education climate, academics are aware of the potential cost of not doing research. This suggests that those who choose not to do research will have solid arguments for that choice. It is clear that there are academics who decide that teaching will permanently displace research. While we would acknowledge their freedom to make this choice, we are concerned that they may be missing out on an experience that could enhance their teaching.

In practice, what may happen is that those who say that teaching leaves them no time for research may well have to write about or research their teaching role for the purpose of demonstrating their continuing competence. Because this requirement is not yet routine, there is perhaps a delay in initiating this type of research or scholarship.

However, there are academics who interpret this discussion as making 'excuses' not to do research:

> For a lot of people, talking about writing is the same as doing it. They see writing as very difficult, with competing demands, which is true, but the task is just doing it. I do not find it interesting to listen to problems and reasons and excuses. . . . They just talk the talk.

Similarly, there are academics who, while acknowledging that making time for research while carrying a heavy teaching load is a 'worry', use more moderate terms to express the importance of not only doing research but also publishing it:

> The only way that you're going to continue to have a rewarding job in here is by reflecting on your experience and practice and putting it out into the public domain where people can comment and give you feedback.

What can you learn from our account of academics' experiences and perspectives on the teaching–research tension?

- There is a teaching–research tension, but it's not the only tension for writers.
- Tension lies in the gap between perceived institutional values and personal values.
- Avoidance leads to uncertainty, insecurity and low self-esteem.
- 'Utility' can, and perhaps should, be balanced by scholarly 'value'.

Only the individual writer can resolve the teaching–research tension. Only individual academics can work out how to balance the utility and scholarly value of their research. Only you can work out how to align your values with those of the scholarly community and calculate the benefit that might bring to both.

The purpose of this section was to shed light on one complex and difficult issue in order to assist those who have not yet fully, or recently, examined internalized teaching–research tensions. We may have identified areas where you would benefit from support:

> Professionals and service users and carers need not only motivation to undertake such writing but also practical support in taking steps necessary to enable this to happen. Such writing, if rooted in critical reflexivity on everyday practice, enriches and informs the continuous development of . . . practice and provides valuable colour and texture to the landscape of the evidence base.
>
> (Waldman, 2005: 980)

Waldman concludes that the 'complexity' of this model is crucial, reminding us that we need more than encouragement, support, motivation or even sanctions and rewards to do research; we need a model for research and writing that is itself complex, in the sense of integrating the different aspects of research, including writing.

The key may be in the individual academic's ability to integrate writing in everyday practice, both cognitively and behaviourally. For those who have not yet done so, we propose, that writing about teaching is one way of achieving this. This could be one way of achieving 'continuous development' not only of content but also of your writing process. The teaching–research tension could itself be a subject for scholarly writing. In the final section we suggest ways in which you can do this, or, if you already do, ways in which you can extend that work.

Teaching–research synergies

I want something that could fit back into my teaching in some way.

Academics are often searching for ways to integrate teaching and research. Writing about your teaching can be a way into writing and need not stop you doing other types of writing, research or scholarship. In fact, writing about teaching may again be a way of transforming a barrier into a lever. This is one way of developing your writing skills, confirming your commitment to writing and generating regular outputs. While Chapter 8 considered how you might reconceptualize writing through teaching, this section explores how you might reconceptualize teaching through writing.

Instead of allowing teaching to drive you away from writing, you can build bridges between the two. If you are a committed teacher, first and foremost, there is the added incentive of writing about a subject you value. You will be motivated to update your skills and knowledge from time to time, and this too can be the subject of writing in your teaching portfolio.

In the current culture of higher education it is assumed that you are a professionally qualified teacher, committed to continually updating your skills. This means that you are likely to have to demonstrate your competencies in the teaching role regularly, throughout your career. Continuing professional development is now expected of you. It may no longer be possible to take anything other than a scholarly approach to teaching.

Guidance on putting together a teaching portfolio will be provided by your discipline, institution or professional body. General guidance is also available (e.g. Morss and Murray, 2005).

Writing for your teaching portfolio

What are the implications of this book/chapter for your teaching?

You could start by writing notes on your responses to [key teaching issues]. If you do not see any, it could be interesting to explain and justify your impressions in a short piece of writing, perhaps even a mini-argument.

These writing activities might, in any case, prompt you to reflect on the directions your reactions are running in. This writing need not be onerous, or detailed, but it can be quite revealing.

You might find it useful to have a more focused discussion about

1   the place of writing in your life at this time; and
2   past, current or potential teaching–research tensions.

This might help you with 'relapse prevention' (covered in Chapter 9) in your academic writing.

Has this chapter consolidated your views or raised new questions?

You could identify and explore questions this chapter has answered or raised for you. This is not intended as a follow on from the first activity; these are suggestions for writing about your teaching in different forms and with different focuses. What is central to all of these prompts is that you use writing to explore, and possibly develop, your thinking about your teaching in relation to your research and writing.

Did our summaries of the experiences of academics in the previous section of this chapter resonate with you?

If so, you could compare your interpretation of the teaching–research tension with ours. If not, you could articulate, in a brief piece of writing that may be as subjective and as theoretical as you wish, for the purposes of this exercise, your definition of teaching–research tensions, drawing on your experiences and/or observations.

Improving goal-setting and adjusting values are complex processes

This is why it might be worth taking time to describe and analyse them in some detail and in writing. In addition, given that change occurs in cycles, there may be value in continuing this type of reflective writing.

Did any point in this or other chapters set you thinking?

Could that be the subject of future study or reading? Have you discussed it with colleagues, before or since? What are the implications for how you balance teaching and research or writing?

What is the 'scholarship of teaching'?

What does this mean? How can you find out more about it? How can you join that scholarly debate? What are the great debates? Who are the participants? How much of this is, or should be, discipline-specific?

Have you used writing strategies described in this book with your students?

Which one(s)? For what purpose? What happened? What do you think that means? What did you learn from that? What literature did you draw on? Which of our references did you follow up? Has this affected your own writing – for example, your writing practices – in any way? Would you use this activity again with your students? With undergraduates only, or could it also have potential for postgraduates? For example, Elbow's writing on freewriting? Document what you did, including your rationale and your observations – what can you add to the debates on student writing? Do you have the basis for a paper on this subject? Could you present at a conference? Which ones? Teaching and learning in higher education conferences, student writing conferences or subject conferences?

These are ways of writing about your teaching for the purposes of developing and demonstrating your understanding and competence. If you want to achieve all of this, you need to give some thought to several questions:

Audience and purpose

- Where do these writings go?
- What is their purpose?
- Who are they for?
- Should anyone else see some/all of your writing?
- What criteria will others bring to your writing about teaching?
- Do your writings contain potential talking points for annual review?
- Or is that the last place you would express some of these ideas?

It is also instructive to write about teaching for publication, demonstrating scholarship of teaching, submitting to peer review in this field as you do in your own. This is another way of putting your ideas to the test. It is also another source of feedback on your ability to construct academic arguments, to supply evidence to support your assertions and to critique other literature.

We have found that academics who undertake a course of study on teaching and learning in higher education are often stimulated by a scholarly approach to this field. Some are surprised to find that there is a literature on this subject at all. Most are quickly engaged by quality research and publications, particularly if these suggest solutions to problems they face, or offer directions for taking their teaching forward. For example, academics studying a masters module on Academic Writing were motivated to try some of the new strategies they had recently learned in their own teaching. They used freewriting with undergraduate classes, for example.

Learning about this or other aspects of the teaching role – by means of a formal course, with seminar discussions, informal conversations, assessment and reflective writing – can help you to make connections between your research and teaching roles (Murray, 2001). Once you see that there is a body of knowledge that you can learn about and that can be related to your research role – in writing for publication – it becomes meaningful. You can also connect your own writing with that of your students. In these ways, writing, as a subject of study, becomes a fulcrum between teaching and

research. Writing about these matters is a means of developing your understanding even further.

This type of course, particularly one on academic writing, prompts you
to reflect explicitly on what you learned about writing – if anything – as an
undergraduate student and to make connections between the experience of
learning as student and as academic:

> The writing process was something I hadn't given much thought to before
> starting the course. . . . One of the first topics explored was how is aca-
> demic writing learned, the answer, certainly within the UK seems to be by
> trial and error. On reflection, I cannot recall being given formal instruc-
> tion on the specifics of academic writing during my undergraduate career.
> This trial and error process was not just exclusively confined to academic
> writing, but extends to all forms of writing. For a skill that is so important,
> particularly in academic life, I am still surprised at how little time is given
> to formally developing writing techniques and the transference of those
> skills to students.
>
> (Murray, 2001: 35)

With regard to writing, module participants identified seven strategies that
had proved useful in their teaching, or writing or both (Murray, 2001: 37):

1 Discussing writing with others.
2 Getting feedback on writing from others.
3 Freewriting (Elbow, 1973).
4 Generative writing (Boice, 1990).
5 Goal setting for writing.
6 Using a framework for writing abstracts (Brown, 1994/95).
7 Discussing feedback with the course tutor.

They identified specific interventions they had started to make in their teaching, resulting from the Academic Writing module (Murray, 2001: 39):

> When I've finished a class and got them to write 50 words on the learning
> from that class.

> I insist that undergraduate classes write in class (5 minutes). This is a
> dramatic change. Prior to this it was lecture discussion notes.

> I use writing in class as a dynamic: writing in different forms, with differ-
> ent purposes, linking back to the assignment, summing up, making links.
> Also with dissertation students: we discuss and I prompt them to write
> there and then.

Many potential teaching–research synergies can stimulate your writing and
your understanding of writing in the learning process.

Where are the potential teaching–writing synergies?

- Testing new knowledge in classroom contexts . . . learning more about writing as you do.
- Discussing writing with postgraduate students – opening up your own knowledge of principles and practices of academic writing to them.
- Directing scholarly attention to what happens in the classroom, analysing teaching and learning in the disciplines.
- Writing can be a vehicle for integrating teaching and research.
- Working on writing with students leading to various learning outcomes.
- Writing to get people to think in more research-oriented ways.
- Writing can be a bridge for bringing all academic activities together.

However, these synergies only occur if you construct them. Only you can create these synergies in the context of your own teaching–writing life. The extent to which your observations and experiences constitute 'research' is a question you need to answer, but there are examples in different fields. The following examples may help you to derive prompts for thinking and writing about teaching and learning in higher education:

> This is both a review of . . . as well as an attempt to place the issue in a practical and reasonable context.
>
> (Ziegler, 2001)

In your writing you can review literature or concepts, framing or finding a 'place' for an issue you feel has not been resolved.

> A theoretical model is offered . . .
>
> (Gavin and Lister, 2001)

You can develop or comment on one or more theoretical models available for teaching in your discipline, or perhaps currently used in other disciplines.

> The author draws upon 30 years of experience in . . .
>
> (Anglin, 1999)

Summarize and critique trends you perceive in teaching and learning during your experience as a higher education teacher.

> This article looks at how . . . There is a discussion of practical skills and training directions . . .
>
> (Pazaratz, 2001)

Describe 'practical skills' and 'training directions' of, for example, research supervisors or external and internal examiners or, more specifically, review the diversification of the doctorate and explore implications for examination of different doctorates in your discipline.

These examples suggest practical ways to stimulate scholarly dialogue to feed your writing. You can write in scholarly ways without waiting until you produce the forms of 'research' that you do in your own discipline.

If you position yourself as a practitioner of higher education teaching, and if these ideas are not common currency in your department or institution, you do not have to navigate this territory alone. Numerous groups and bodies support research and writing on teaching and learning in higher education. Accessing their materials will help you to integrate your teaching and research roles:

> Further complexity is brought into the picture once we start to unpick the differences between research which is academic-led and research which is practitioner-led or practice-based. In these models, research and practice are no longer conceived as isolated but as integrated activities that borrow from each other, inform each other and support each other.
>
> (Furlong and Oancea, 2005: 8)

Writing continues to be a mode of inquiry, in teaching and learning as in your 'home' discipline. Writing keeps you making connections at the individual, not only institutional or theoretical, levels.

Checklist

- Don't take on too much – this is easier said than done.
- Align your definition of 'too much' with others'. Talk to your head of department.
- If you only get a 'buzz' from teaching, review your definition of 'research'.
- Establish what value research has for you, the university, your profession.
- Find or create synergies between your teaching and research (see Chapter 3).
- Start a teaching portfolio and write about your teaching in any form.
- If you already have a teaching portfolio, consider broadening the contents.
- Identify aspects of teaching and learning that you'd like to know more about.
- Write about your practice – make links with the literature.
- Write a scholarly paper about your teaching and submit it to a journal.

11

Advancing and retreating

The essential dynamic of academic writing

Introduction • Risk and opportunity in academic writing • Understanding your own writing context • Becoming an academic writer • Understanding your own writing processes • Not at any cost • Conclusion

Introduction

We present two models in this chapter that we hope will help you to integrate many of the ideas that we have proposed and discussed throughout this book in order to situate your academic writing and to manage the processes that it requires. Firstly, the structural model of academic writing (Figure 11.1) draws together the themes that we have explored earlier and also extends that exploration, particularly by focusing on the moderators that can influence whether you transform your initial writing efforts into productive writing outputs.

We emphasize that even though academic life is characterized by certain contexts and conditions, it is also possible to change and influence those contexts in order to support and sustain your writing. The process model of academic writing (Figure 11.2) reiterates the rhythms of writing that have also been an essential theme in this book. And it provides examples of the kinds of progressive unfolding of writing-related activities. Again, this model draws together ideas that have been invoked in earlier chapters in order to set out more clearly what we mean when we talk about active and reflective phases of writing and the essential process of moving back and forth from one mode of engagement to the other. You have already seen that academic writing requires an engagement with a series of activities, many of which are very different from each other and many of which require activation at different stages in the writing process. The paradoxes that we explored in Chapter 1 echo again in Figure 11.2, and we hope that you can readily identify some of the tensions, pulls and contradictions that these different activities might present for you.

While many 'writers on writing' have already and regularly pointed out that there are different phases of writing, and many mention the iterative nature of the writing process, we have tried to enrich these established insights by illuminating the 'advance-retreat' dynamic in a way that captures a range of associated, unfolding behaviours. Here in this final chapter we capture and display this dynamic in a process model. It is defined by several iterations of the 'advance-retreat' dynamic.

Essentially, the models we present in this chapter will help visually to map out, link up and extend the many interconnected ideas about academic writing that we have presented earlier.

Risk and opportunity in academic writing

So far, we have shared and explored insights, ideas and strategies that many writers have found useful and productive in helping to develop academic writing strategies. As you will have seen, some of what we have shared relates to broad conceptualizations of what writing is (and we have presented it as an iterative process that involves advances and retreats of different kinds); some relates to specific individual and institutional strategies that directly feed writing fluency and the production of written text (for example, writers' retreats, writing programmes and writers' groups), and some relates to the ways in which it is possible to negotiate time and space for writing in the context of your life. We have tried to approach the process of writing in quite comprehensive ways, referring not just to the mechanics of academic rhetoric, but also to working contexts and processes that might help you to become an insightful and self-aware writer of academic work. But given that academic writing operates in a context of unequal power and requires at least some risk on the part of writers themselves, this knowledge and these ideas and insights, while potentially helpful, will not equip you for every eventuality.

Even when you have considered, selected and activated some of the strategies and activities that we have suggested in this book so far, they will not protect you completely from the pitfalls and hazards associated with the writing process in academia. On the positive side, though, neither will they prepare you for all the possibilities and potential that your writing may also contain.

From working with many academics on developing their writing, our words of caution are these: no matter how well equipped you are, or no matter how able you are planning to become in tackling the challenges of academic writing, it still carries risks. But our words of encouragement in Part I still stand. That is, that even though there are risks, they are generally worth taking. Whenever you write, you run the risk that you will be unsupported, resented, unrewarded, inappropriately criticized or even belittled. But you also create the possibility that you will begin new conversations, forge new links, articulate ideas in new ways or contexts, and gain the endorsement and satisfaction that come from having your ideas heard. You run the risk that it will take you away from other important priorities in your life, but you create the possibility that it will uncover meaningful priorities for you. You run the risk that you will incur costs that may not be redeemable at a later date (like time with your children or your partner, like the pursuit of other goals that are not related to writing), but you also create the possibility that it will give rise to new freedoms and new options for you. You run the sometimes significant risk that anonymous reviewers will berate you, misinterpret your words and criticize you for things you did not say, or for things you did say, but you also create the possibility that you will draw attention to interesting and important work, and that you will make that contribution beyond your classrooms or the limits of your local network.

If you understand the odds and the balance between opportunities and risks in your writing, then you can reduce your chances of 'getting burned', but you will not completely eliminate them. So be prepared for the hazards and risks that academic writing causes you to run, but don't shy away from taking (and continuing to take) the leap. This preparedness will make you find ways of progressing even when you have been discouraged, and to know when you need to stop for a while to regroup and to reconsider your approach or even to detach yourself from the writing process altogether. Importantly, as well as becoming strategic and understanding how to 'play the academic writing game', equipping yourself with an awareness of the risks and opportunities also creates a framework in which you may engage actively and deliberately with the processes and rules of scholarship. Simply put, academic writing sharpens your practice as a scholar.

Understanding your own writing context

But of course we cannot talk about risks, hazards and opportunities as if they were the same things for all academic writers. Quite the contrary, your own combination of risks and hazards may be unique to you, as may be the power relationships and dynamics that contribute to your working context. We propose, however, that at least some of the features that are outlined in Figure 11.1 are also likely to be a feature of your environment. This diagram represents a framework that you might use to 'deconstruct' the contexts in which you write. By combining insights from theories of motivation and engagement (e.g. Porter and Lawler, 1968; Czikzsentimihalyi, 1990 and Goleman, 1995) and by applying these ideas to the interrogation of academics' accounts of their writing triggers, prohibitors and moderators, we identify a range of writing-related issues and conditions and we show the ways in which they are likely to be connected.

It is possible to differentiate between factors that are likely to encourage (or prohibit) the initiation of your writing, and factors that facilitate the translation (or not) of these efforts into productive, useful, professionally developing outputs.

The development of this model is based on both theory and evidence that there are common triggers and blocks that facilitate and prohibit the initiation of writing; and that there are commonly invoked moderators (both individual and environmental) that can influence whether writing activity leads to productive outputs.

In addition, there are different kinds of rewards associated with writing, which can broadly be divided into two categories: instrinsic and extrinsic (see Watson, 2002). Our qualitative analysis of accounts of academic writing suggest also that there are feedback loops which involve analysing the rewards to which writing activity has given rise in the past, in a way that guides future decisions about writing. This echoes the principles associated with general theories of work motivation (see, for example, Morley et al., 2004) and applies those ideas to the specific activity of academic writing.

Becoming an academic writer

What the model also attempts to emphasize is that the process of 'becoming a writer' is not something that happens to you once and then subsequently defines you for ever more. Writing is an activity that can start or stop at any time depending on the particular combination of choices, activities, priorities and conditions operating within your life. Sometimes these starts and stops serve to feed writing and respond to the rhythms of your work and your life. But sometimes they are more problematic than that. Just as non-writers can become active writers, so is it possible for active and sometimes even very successful writers to abandon their work. To build a sustained approach to academic writing then, it is useful to analyse what your own personal triggers and blocks might be, and to understand the nature of the individual and environmental moderators that relate to your professional experience, remembering that you can influence them through your own insights and decisions, and recognizing that they are likely to change over time.

We think that it is also useful to think deliberately and explicitly about the kinds of rewards you value most and the ones that are most likely to be connected to your writing efforts and outputs. The possibility that some of these will be rewards that come from your external environment and that others will be intrinsic to your own experience, esteem and satisfaction, is something that is also worth your attention and reflection. The rewards you receive and those that you value most, are likely to have a strong influence on your commitment to writing and to the scholarship and engagement that this requires.

So the factors that we highlight in Figure 11.1 and the interrelationships between them are potentially very important for you. They may be able to help you to diagnose your own writing context and to create scaffolding that will help you sustain your writing, if on examination, you decide that such scaffolding does not exist.

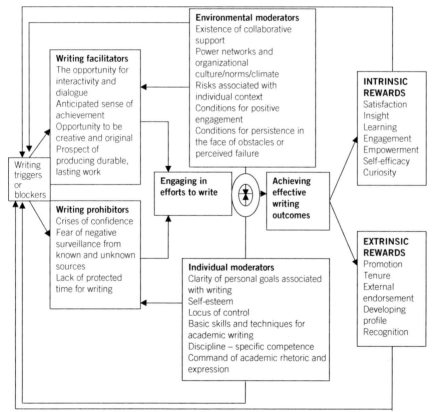

Figure 11.1 A structural model of academic writing: framing your academic writing context
Adapted from Moore (2003)

Understanding your own writing processes

The feeling of going forwards and then backwards again is something that takes getting used to. Zerubavel (1999) notes that revising, revisiting and re-examining written work is not something that we are typically trained to do as undergraduates or even at higher levels in our academic development. Besides, the 'retreat' mode of academic writing is characterized by a form of engagement that tends not to prevail in many Western cultures and work climates, not least academic ones. Retreating is taught infrequently and arguably contrasts with the norms and values that reign in academic settings. And, because we consider it to be an essential, balancing dynamic which moderates and nourishes the active, progressive phase of advance, most people need at least some training or group support in order to get used to it.

We hope by now that you have many ideas about how you can do this and about what that means for your writing processes, development and productivity. Scheduling in time for retreat (see Chapter 1), planning to get engaged in a retreat phase (see Chapter 3) and retreating in order to advance (see Chapter 5), are all ways in which you can build retreating activites into your academic writing.

Figure 11.2 shows that successive stages of advance and retreat might themselves also be characterized by different kinds of activities. Certain stages of advance require unbridled brainstorming, while later stages might require the active integration of the critique of others into your writing. Certain stages of retreat require listening to other perspectives on your writing for the first time, while subsequent stages of retreat may require a re-examination of those critiques and insights in ways that might even cause you to come full circle. Figure 11.2 is a simplification of the iterative process that may of course be much more complex and have many more iterations than we have presented. Advance can start with many possible activities that we have not identified in the model. (Hjortshoj, 2001, refers to 'prewriting' as anything that prepares us to write or that happens in advance of an active writing process. This could arguably be anything we have ever done, thought or felt.) Similarly, the real experiences of writers mean that the 'release' of your writing or submission for publication, sets a whole new series of iterations in motion that are also not displayed in Figure 11.2.

The writing processes in which you engage, like those we have identified in Figure 11.2, will impact on the writing contexts in which you operate (as defined by the features displayed in Figure 11.1). You may find that the successful publication of a piece of writing serves to introduce you to a new community of writers/scholars that significantly shifts your writing context. You may discover that aspects of your context, like the establishment of a strong mentor, can impact on the processes you use to write. You might discover that the intrinsic sense of achievement that you experience in the production and

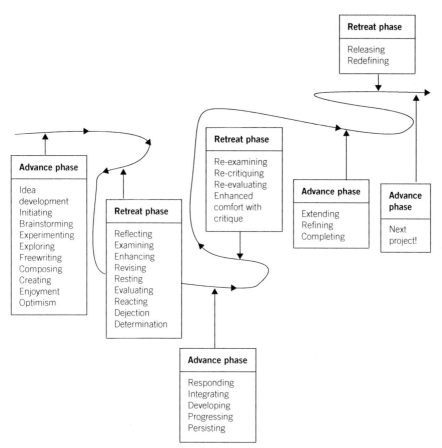

Figure 11.2 A process model of academic writing: tracking your academic writing processes

successful publication of written output causes you to persist with future projects where without that reward, you might have been less tenacious in the development of your work and your ideas.

Note that as a backdrop to each of the diagrams presented above, there are three overarching strategic dynamics (Pettigrew and Whipp, 1991) that you might consider applying to your writing: the **context** within which you write, your writing **processes** and the **content** of your writing. Simple questions about why you write, how you write and what you write might be a useful starting point for analysing the other dynamics that we present in the figures in this chapter.

Not at any cost

At the very beginning of this book we highlighted that career development in academia is a process that influences and is influenced by your academic writing. But you probably don't need us to tell you that. Many discussions in academia focus on the rights and wrongs of the rules associated with decisions relating to reward, promotion and tenure and the ways in which such rules are applied. Many commentators argue that academic institutions reflect the inequities and inconsistencies of organizations in general, and that the idea that meritocratic principles apply is naïve in the extreme. It is in this context that the pursuit of rewards like tenure or promotion is both competitive and fraught. Acker and Armenti (2004) have recently commented that 'the process by which tenure is obtained has become a tormenting ritual that seems to have gone out of control' and say that they 'see people who are already committed to excellence and productivity, risking their health and happiness to arrive at even higher and ever more mystifying performance standards' (p. 19).

Academic writing and its fickle promises of external reward should not be pursued at all costs. Very few things are important enough to risk health and well-being. We hope that we have encouraged you to recognize that you can become a productive and successful academic writer without incurring that risk.

Conclusion

The purpose of this final discussion has not only been to synthesize and crystallize the insights, advice, strategies and ideas that have been presented in this book. It has also taken these ideas further and attempted to situate them in the structural and process models of academic writing that have been presented. We have represented academic writing as something that incorporates many paradoxes and challenges that once explored and examined, ultimately become easier to manage than might otherwise have been the case. We have explained how certain levels of chaos are inevitable and necessary during academic writing tasks, and have encouraged you to use this chaos in a way that builds your ideas and insights, but in a way that does not prohibit the imposition of structure and form on your writing processes.

We have incorporated the practical implications of the iterative dynamics of writing. We have emphasized that building up a social support system to facilitate the ebbs and flows of writing is often necessary, perhaps particularly at crucial stages of the writing process.

Remember also that healthy habits may fail, effective patterns may break and writing strategies may work well in one context but not in others. In academic writing there seems to be a fairly common need for people to start and stop, to jump in and jump out, to find their own rhythms of advancing and retreating. A healthy, productive, satisfying and pleasurable approach to academic writing often simply means being able to recognize and become comfortable with the ebbs and flows of the processes involved.

Writing processes expressed by other authors all build in the notion that there are different stages in the writing process. Writers who have commented insightfully on this process include those whose work we have regularly invoked throughout this book. Hjortshoj names the phases of writing as prewriting, composing, revising, editing and release. Zerubavel talks about getting started, moving along and closing. We believe that the iterative nature of writing needs to be more explicitly recognized both in the theory and the practice of academic writing. In order to utilize the benefits to which revisability gives rise, it needs to be embraced, not avoided. These dynamics are why academic writing can be so fascinating and professionally helpful. What should be celebrated rather than lamented is this inherent opportunity always to revisit, to refine, to re-orientate, to redisplay and to re-examine the work we have done or are doing. In many ways, this represents some of the essential aspects of learning. It is often the very writing dynamics that are frustrating and sometimes prohibitive that may in the end be what makes academic life so full of potential for continued growth, learning and development.

Very few things are linear in nature, but there is a symmetry to most things as there is in writing. For every up there may be a down, for every step forward you may also need to step back, for every win there may be a loss. Recognizing and embracing this can help your writing motivation to sustain itself even under fire or when confidence and self-assuredness are low. Balance, reciprocation, isolation and togetherness, immersion and dispersion – all of these are not just features of academic writing, they are the conditions of academic life.

Bibliography

Acker, S. and Armenti, C. (2004) Sleepless in academia, *Gender and Education*, 16(1): 3–24.

Anand, V., Glick, W.H, and Manz, C. (2002) Thriving on the knowledge of outsiders: tapping organizational social capital, *Academy of Management Executive*, 16(1): 87–101.

Anglin, J. (1999) The uniqueness of child and youth care: a personal perspective, *Child and Youth Care Forum*, 28(2): 143–50.

Baldwin, C. and Chandler, G.E. (2002) Improving faculty publication output: the role of a writing coach, *Journal of Professional Nursing*, 18(1): 8–15.

Bandura, A. (1977) Towards a unifying theory of behaviour change, *Psychological Review*, 84: 191–215.

Barron, F. and Harrington, D. (1981) Creativity, intelligence and personality, in M. Rosenweigh and L. Porter (eds) *Annual Review of Psychology*, 32: 439–76. Palo Alto, CA: Annual Reviews.

Bean, J.C. (2001) *Engaging Ideas: The Professor's Guide to Integrated Writing, Critical Thinking, and Active Learning in the Classroom*. San Francisco: Jossey-Bass.

Becker, H.S. (1986) *Writing for Social Scientists: How to Start and Finish Your Thesis, Book or Article*. Chicago: University of Chicago Press.

Berger, R.M. (1990) Getting published: a mentoring program for social work faculty, *Social Work*, 35(1): 69–71.

Blanton, H., Pelham, B., DeHart, T. and Carvallo, M. (2001) Overconfidence as dissonance reduction, *Journal of Experimental and Social Psychology*, 37: 373–85.

Bloom, L.Z. (1985) Anxious writers in context: graduate school and beyond, in M. Rose (ed.) *When a Writer Can't Write*. New York: Guilford Press, pp. 119–33.

Boice, R. (1982) Increasing the writing productivity of 'blocked' academicians, *Behavior Research and Therapy*, 20: 197–207.

Boice, R. (1987) Is released-time an effective device for faculty development?, *Research in Higher Education*, 26: 311–26.

Boice, R. (1989) Procrastination, busyness and bingeing, *Behavior Research and Therapy*, 27: 605–11.

Boice, R. (1990) *Professors as Writers: A Self-Help Guide to Productive Writing*. Stillwater, OK: New Forums.

Boice, R. and Jones, F. (1984) Why academicians don't write, *Journal of Higher Education*, 55(5): 20–34.

Boud, D. and Walker, D. (1998) Promoting reflection in professional courses: the challenge of context, *Studies in Higher Education*, 23(2): 191–206.

Boyer, E. (1990) *Scholarship Reconsidered: Priorities of the Professoriate*. Princeton, NJ: Carnegie Foundation.

Bradford, A.N. (1983) Cognitive immaturity and remedial college writers, in J.N. Hays, P.A. Roth, J.R. Ramsay and R.D. Foulke (eds) *The Writer's Mind: Writing as a Mode of Thinking*. Urbana, Ill: National Council of Teachers of English.

Brandreth, G. (2006) Diary, *The Spectator*, 18 March.

Brown, R. (1994/95) Write first time, *Literati Newsline*, special issue: 1–8.

Cameron, J. (1999) *The Right to Write*. New York: MacMillan.

Canagarajah, A.S. (2002) *A Geopolitics of Academic Writing*. Pittsburg: University of Pittsburg Press.

Carlson, G.-E. and Ludwig-Beymer, P. (1997) Stimulating peers to publish: the role of staff development, *Journal of Nursing Staff Development*, 13(6): 314–18.

Cayton, M.K. (1990) What happens when things go wrong: women and writing blocks, *Journal of Advanced Composition*, 10: 321–38.

Chandler, J., Barry, J. and Clark, H. (2002) Stressing academe: the wear and tear of the New Public Management, *Human Relations*, 55(9): 1051–69.

Coniam, D. (2004) Concordancing yourself: a personal exploration of academic writing, *Language Awareness*, 13(1): 49–55.

Cooper, C. (2000) *Theories of Organizational Stress*. Oxford: Oxford University Press.

Csikszentmihalyi, M. (1990) *Flow: The Psychology of Optimal Experience*. New York: Harper and Row.

Daily, L.Z., Lovett, M.C. and Reder, L.M. (2001) Modeling individual differences in working memory performance: a source activation account, *Cognitive Science*, 25: 315–53.

Daly, J.A. and Miller, M.D. (1975) The empirical development of an instrument to measure writing apprehension, *Research in the Teaching of English*, 9: 242–9.

DeBeaugrande, R. (1982) Cognitive processes and technical writing: developmental foundations, *Journal of Technical Writing and Communications*, 12: 121–45.

de Janasz, S., Sullivan, S. and Whiting, V. (2003) Mentor networks and career success, *Academy of Management Executive*, 17(4): 78–91.

Derricourt, R. (1996) *An Author's Guide to Scholarly Publishing*. Princeton: Princeton University Press.

Doyle, C. and Hind, P. (1998) Occupational stress, burnout and job status in female academics, *Gender, Stress and Organization*, 5(2): 67–82.

Dweck, C.S. and Elliott, E.S. (1983) Achievement motivation, in P.H. Mussen and E.M. Hetherington (eds) *Handbook of Child Psychology*, Vol. 4: *Social and Personality Development*. New York: Wiley, pp. 643–91.

Eckert, C. and Stacey, M. (1998) Fortune favours only the prepared mind: why sources of inspiration are essential for continuing creativity, *Creativity and Innovation Management*, 7(1): 9–16.

Elbow, P. (1973) *Writing Without Teachers*. Oxford: Oxford University Press.

Elbow, P. (1981) *Writing with Power*. New York: Oxford University Press.

Elbow, P. and Belanoff, P. (2000) *A Community of Writers: A Workshop Course in Writing*. London: McGraw-Hill.

Ensher, E.A., Murphy, S. and Sullivan, S.E. (2002) Reel women: lessons from female TV executives on managing work and real life, *Academy of Management Executive*, 16(2): 106–21

Faigley, L. and Witte, S. (1981) Analysing revision, *College Composition and Communication*, 32(4): 400–14.

Festinger, L. (1958) The motivating effect of cognitive dissonance, in L. Gardner (ed.) *Assessment of Human Motives*. New York: Holt, pp. 69–85.

Fisher, C.D. and Yuan, A. (1998) What motivates employees?, *International Journal of Human Resource Management*, 9: 516–28.

Fisher, S. (1995) *Stress in Academic Life.* Buckingham: Open University Press.

Fletcher, R.H. and Fletcher, S.W. (2003) The effectiveness of journal peer review, in F. Godlee and T. Jefferson (eds) *Peer Review in the Health Sciences,* 2nd edn. London: BMJ Publishing Group, pp. 62–75.

Flower, L. and Hayes, J. (1977) Problem solving strategies and the writing process, *College English,* 39(4): 449–61.

Freidman, B. (1993) *Writing Past Dark: Envy, Fear, Distraction and Other Dilemmas in the Writer's Life.* New York: Harper.

Furlong, J. and Oancea, A. (2005) *Assessing Quality in Applied and Practice-based Educational Research: A Framework for Discussion.* Oxford: Oxford University Department of Educational Studies. http://www.bera.ac.uk/pdfs/Qualitycriteria.pdf (accessed 26 February 2006).

Gainen, J. (1993) A writing support program for junior women faculty, *New Directions for Teaching and Learning,* 53: 91–100.

Gavin, J. and Lister, S. (2001) The strategic use of sports and fitness activities for promoting psychosocial skill development in childhood and adolescence, *Journal of Child and Youth Care Work,* 20: 325–39.

Germano, W. (2001) *Getting It Published: A Guide for Scholars Serious about Serious Books.* Chicago: University of Chicago Press.

Gibaldi, J. (1999) *MLA Handbook for Writers of Research Papers.* New York: The Modern Language Association.

Goleman, D. (1995) *Emotional Intelligence: Why It Can Matter More than IQ.* London: Bloomsbury.

Gordon, R.S. (2004) *The Librarian's Guide to Writing for Publication.* Lanham, MD: Scarecrow Press.

Grant, B. and Knowles, S. (2000) Flights of imagination: academic writers be(com)ing writers, *International Journal for Academic Development,* 5(1): 6–19.

Gruber, H. (1988) Inching our way up Mount Olympus: the evolving systems approach to creative thinking, in R. Sternberg (ed). *The Nature of Creativity.* Cambridge: Cambridge University Press, pp. 243–70.

Grzybowski S.C.W. et al. (2003) A physician peer support writing group, *Family Medicine,* 35(3): 195–201.

Haines, D.D., Newcomer, S. and Raphael, J. (1997) *Writing Together: How to Transform Your Writing in a Writing Group.* New York: Pedigree.

Harris, C., Daniels, K. and Briner, R.B. (2003) A daily diary study of goals and affective wellbeing at work, *Journal of Occupational and Organizational Psychology,* 76: 401–10.

Hartley, J. (2005) How to referee a paper, *PsyPag Quarterly Newsletter,* 56: 15–20 (British Psychological Society).

Hartley, J. and Branthwaite, A. (1989) The psychologist as wordsmith: a questionnaire study of the writing strategies of productive British psychologists, *Higher Education,* 18: 423–52.

Hekelman, F.P., Gilchrist, V., Zyzanski, S.J., Glover, P. and Olness, K. (1995) An educational intervention to increase faculty publication productivity, *Family Medicine,* 27(4): 255–9.

Henninger, D.E. and Nolan, M.T. (1998) A comparative evaluation of two educational strategies to promote publication by nurses, *Journal of Continuing Education in Nursing,* 29(2): 79–84.

Hjortshoj, K. (2001) *Understanding Writing Blocks.* Oxford: Oxford University Press.

Hofstede, G. (1982) *Culture's Consequences: International Differences in Work Related Values*. Beverly Hills, CA: Sage.

Hofstede, G. (1991) *Cultures and Organisations: Software of the Mind*. London: McGraw-Hill.

Holkeboer, W.L. (1986) *Creative Agony: Why Writers Suffer*. Bristol, Ind.: Wyndham Hall Press.

Hughes, A.R., Kirk, A.F. and MacIntyre, P.D. (2002) Exercise consultation improves exercise adherence in phase IV cardiac rehabilitation, *Journal of Cardiopulmonary Rehabilitation*, 22: 421–5.

Hull, G. (1985) Research on error and correction, in B. McClelland and T. Donovan (eds) *Perspectives on Research and Scholarship in Composition*. New York: Modern Language Association of America, pp. 162–84.

Ilgen, D.R. and Davis C.A. (2000) Bearing bad news: reactions to negative performance feedback, *Applied Psychology: An International Review*, 3: 550–65.

Jensen, E. (1995) *The Learning Brain*. San Diego, CA: The Brain Store.

Johnson, P.E., Grazioli, S., Jamal, K. and Berryman, R.G. (2001) Detecting deception: adversarial problem solving in a low base-rate world, *Cognitive Science*, 25: 355–92.

Johnson, R. (2000) The authority of the student evaluation questionnaire, *Teaching in Higher Education*, 5(4): 417–34.

Kirk, A.F., Mutrie, N. and Fisher, B.M. (2004) Promoting and maintaining physical activity in people with type 2 diabetes, *American Journal of Preventive Medicine*, 27: 289–96.

Kluger, A.N. and DeNisi, A. (1996) The effects of feedback interventions on performance: a historical review, a meta-analysis and a preliminary feedback intervention theory, *Psychological Bulletin*, 119: 254–84.

Kohn, A. (1993) *Punished by Rewards: The Trouble with Gold Stars, Incentive Plans, A's, Praise and Other Bribes*. Boston: Houghton-Mifflin.

Krebs Hirsch, S. and Kummerow, J.M. (1990) *Introduction to Type in Organisations*. Palo Alto, CA: Consulting Psychologists Press.

Kroll, B. (1978) Cognitive egocentrism and the problem of audience awareness in written discourse, *Research in the Teaching of English*, 12(3): 209–81.

Lankau, M.J. and Scandura, T.A. (2002) An investigation of personal learning in mentoring relationships: content, antecedents, and consequences, *Academy of Management Journal*, 45(4): 779–90.

Lawrence, M.M. and Folcik, M.A. (1996) Writing for publication, *Journal of Nursing Staff Development*, 12(6): 289–93.

Lee, A. and Boud, D. (2003) Writing groups, change and academic identity: research development as local practice, *Studies in Higher Education*, 28(2): 187–200.

Levine, M. (2004) *The Myth of Laziness*. New York: Simon and Schuster.

Lock, S. (1986) *A Difficult Balance: Editorial Peer Review in Medicine*. Philadelphia: ISA Press.

Loughlan, C. and Mutrie, N. (1995) Conducting an exercise consultation: guidelines for health professionals, *Journal of the Institute of Health Education*, 33: 78–82.

Luey, B. (2002) *Handbook for Academic Authors*. Cambridge: Cambridge University Press.

Marcus, B.H. and Simkin, L.R. (1994) The transtheoretical model: applications to exercise behaviour, *Medicine, Science, Sport and Exercise*, 24: 1400–4.

McClelland, D.C. (1961) *The Achieving Society*. Princeton, NJ: Van Nostrand.

McGrail, M.R., Rickard, C.M. and Jones, R. (2006) Publish or perish: a systematic review of interventions to increase academic publication rates, *Higher Education Research and Development*, 25(1): 19–35.

McVeigh, C., Moyle, K., Forrester, K., Chaboyer, W., Patterson, E. and St John, W. (2002) Publication syndicates: in support of nursing scholarship, *Journal of Continuing Education in Nursing*, 33(2): 63–6.

Miller, B.K. and Muhlenkamp, A. (1989) Teaching students how to publish in nursing journals: a group approach, *Journal of Nursing Education*, 28(8): 379–81.

Miller, W.R. and Rollnick, S. (2002) *Motivational Interviewing: Preparing People for Change*, 2nd edn. London: Guildford Press.

Moore, S. (1995) *Intensive Writing Program, Progress Reports*. Melbourne: Victoria University of Technology Collaborative Research Group Scheme.

Moore, S. (2003) Writers' retreats for academics: exploring and increasing the motivation to write, *Journal of Further and Higher Education*, 7(3): 333–43.

Moore, S. and Kuol, N. (2005) Students evaluating teachers: exploring the importance of faculty reaction to feedback on teaching, *Teaching in Higher Education*, 10(1): 57–73.

Moore, S. and Murphy, M. (2005) *How to be a Student: 100 Great Ideas and Practical Habits for Students Everywhere*. Buckingham: Open University Press.

Morley, M., Moore, S., Heraty, N., Linehan, M. and MacCurtain, S. (2004) *Principles of Organisational Behaviour: An Introductory Text*. Dublin: Gill and MacMillan.

Morss, K. and Murray, R. (2001) Researching academic writing within a structured programme: insights and outcomes, *Studies in Higher Education*, 26(1): 35–51.

Morss, K. and Murray, R. (2005) *Teaching at University: A Guide for Postgraduates*. London: Sage.

Mullin, W.J. (1989) Qualitative thinking and writing in the hard sciences, in P. Connolly and T. Vilardi (eds) *Writing to Learn in Mathematics and Science*. New York: Teachers' College Press.

Murray, R. (2001) Integrating teaching and research through writing development for students and staff, *Active Learning in Higher Education*, 2(1): 31–45.

Murray, R. (2002) *How to Write a Thesis*. Buckingham: Open University Press.

Murray, R. (2004) *Writing for Academic Journals*. Maidenhead: Open University Press.

Murray R. (2006) Writing articles, books and presentations, in N. Gilbert (ed.) *The Postgraduate Guidebook: Essential Skills for a Career in the Social Sciences*. London: Sage.

Murray, R. and MacKay, G. (1998) Supporting academic development in public output: reflections and propositions, *International Journal for Academic Development*, 3(1): 54–63.

Nelson, V. (1993) *On Writer's Block*. Boston: Houghton Mifflin.

Norman, R. (1995) The scholarly journal and intellectual sensorium, in J.M. Moxley and L.T. Lenker (eds) *The Politics and Processes of Scholarship*. Westport, Conn: Greenwood.

O'Neill, G., Moore, S. and McMullin, B. (eds) (2005) *Emerging Issues in the Practice of University Teaching and Learning*. Dublin: All Ireland Society for Higher Education.

Ostrowski, P.M. and Bartel, S. (1985) Assisting practitioners to publish through the use of support groups, *Journal of Counselling and Development*, 63(8): 510–11.

Page-Adams, D., Cheng, L.-C., Cogineni, A. and Shen, C.-Y. (1995) Establishing a group to encourage writing for publication among doctoral students, *Journal of Social Work Education*, 31(3): 402–7.

Pazaratz, D. (2001) Defining and describing the child and youth care worker's role in residential treatment, *Journal of Child and Youth Care*, 14(3): 67–77.

Pettigrew, A. and Whipp, R. (1991) *Managing Change for Competitive Success.* Oxford: Blackwell.

Pinder, C. (1998) *Work Motivation in Organisational Behaviour.* New Jersey: Prentice-Hall.

Pololi, L., Knight, S. and Dunn, K. (2004) Facilitating scholarly writing in academic medicine, *Journal of General Internal Medicine*, 19(1): 64–8.

Porter, L. and Lawler, E. (1968) *Managerial Attitudes and Performance.* Homewood, Ill: Dorsey Press.

Raftopoulos, A. (2001) Is perception informationally encapsulated? The issue of the theory-ladenness of perception, *Cognitive Science*, 25: 423–51.

Ramsden, P. (1994) Describing and explaining research productivity, *Higher Education*, 28(2): 207–26.

Rankin, E. (2001) *The Work of Writing: Insights and Strategies for Academics and Professionals.* San Francisco: Jossey-Bass.

Ritchie, S.M. and Rigano, D.L. (2001) Researcher-participant positioning in classroom research, *Qualitative Studies in Education*, 14(6): 741–56.

Runco, M.A. (2004a) Creativity, *Annual Review of Psychology*, 55: 657–87.

Runco, M.A. (2004b) *Critical Creative Processes.* London: Eurospan.

Scneider, P. (2003) *Writing Alone and With Others.* New York: Oxford University Press.

Skelton, J. (1994) Analysis of the structure of original research papers: an aid to writing original papers for publication, *British Journal of General Practice*, 44: 455–9.

Sommers, P.S., Muller, J.H., Bailiff, P.J. and Stephens, G.G. (1996) Writing for publication: a workshop to prepare faculty as medical writers, *Family Medicine*, 28(9): 650–4.

Stern, P.M. (1998) In-house peer review: the writing support group, *Health Care for Women International*, 19(3): 177–8.

Suchan, J. (2004) Writing, authenticity and knowledge creation: why I write and you should too, *Journal of Business Communication*, 41: 302–15.

Truss, L. (2003) *Eats, Shoots and Leaves: The Zero Tolerance Approach to Punctuation.* London: Profile Books.

Turk, C. and Kirkman, J. (1998) *Effective Writing: Improving Scientific, Technical and Business Communication.* London: E & F.N. Spon.

Van den Berghe, P. (1970) *Academic Gamesmanship.* New York: Abelard-Schuman.

Vincent, A. and Seymour, J. (1994) Mentoring among female executives, *Women in Management Review*, 9(7): 15–20.

Vittorini, E. (1959) *Italian Short Stories II.* London: Penguin, p. 61.

Von Eckardt, B. (2001) Multidisciplinarity and cognitive science, *Cognitive Science*, 25: 453–70.

Wagner, U., Gais, S., Haider, H., Verleger, R. and Born, J. (2004) Sleep inspires insight, *Nature*, 427: 352–5.

Waldman, J. (2005) Using evaluative research to support practitioners and service users in undertaking reflective writing for public dissemination, *British Journal of Social Work*, 35(6): 975–81.

Walter, C.B., Swinnen, S.P., Dounskaia, N. and Van Langendonk, H. (2001) Systematic error in the organization of physical action, *Cognitive Science*, 25: 393–422.

Watson, T.J. (2002) *Organising and Managing Work: Organisational, Managerial and Strategic Behaviour in Theory and Practice.* Essex: Prentice-Hall.

Weller, A.C. (2001) *Editorial Peer Review: Its Strengths and Weaknesses.* Medford, NJ: Information Today.

White, R.W. (1959) Motivation reconsidered: the concept of competence, *Psychological Review*, 66: 297–333.

Zerubavel, E. (1999) *The Clockwork Muse: A Practical Guide to Writing Theses, Dissertations and Books*. Cambridge, Mass.: Harvard University Press.

Ziegler, D. (2001) To hold, or not to hold . . . Is that the right question?, *Residential Treatment for Children and Youth*, 18(4): 33–45.

Zinsser, W. (1980) *On Writing Well*. New York: Harper and Row.

INDEX

Related books from Open University Press
Purchase from www.openup.co.uk or order through your local bookseller

---

A GENTLE GUIDE TO RESEARCH METHODS
Gordon Rugg and Marian Petrie

This book consists of "things students wish someone had told them before they started research". Most of these involve advice about the 'big picture' and 'small picture' of research. Many students are unaware of how to get the most out of their research, whether in career terms or in terms of asking good research questions which will lead to interesting findings. This book deals in detail with this question. It also deals with how to move from the big picture to a specific research question and research design: these issues are covered well in many other books, but are seldom located in relation to the big picture.

At a practical level, the book goes into detail about issues which are often overlooked in research methods books, and shows how these link with deeper theoretical issues: for instance, how reformulating a questionnaire item from a yes/no answer into a linear scale can drastically reduce the sample size required for a study, and also how this has methodological advantages in terms of measurement theory.

Contents
Preamble – Acknowledgements – About the authors – Contents page – Introduction – About research – Research design – Generic advice – Data collection – Data analysis – The end game – Bibliography – Glossary – Sources of Quotations – Index.

256pp   0 335 21927 6 (Paperback)   0 335 21928 4 (Hardback)

WRITING FOR ACADEMIC JOURNALS

Rowena Murray

Whether writing the first draft or the final draft, this book enables and inspires academics to develop their own writing strategies and goals.

Lorna Gillies, Lecturer, University of Leicester

Our experience is that Rowena's practical approach works for busy academic staff. Not only does it enable them to increase their publication output and meet deadlines, but it boosts enthusiasm for writing and stimulates creative thinking.

Kate Morss, Director, Centre for Academic Practice,
Queen Margaret University College, Edinburgh, UK

This approach provides scientists with a systematic step-by-step method of producing a paper for publication. The approach streamlines the process and provides strategies for overcoming barriers. Feedback from the professions using the approach was excellent.

Dr Mary Newton, Greater Glasgow Primary Care NHS Trust

This book unpacks the process of writing academic papers. It tells readers what good papers look like and how they can be written.

Busy academics must develop productive writing practices quickly. No one has time for trial and error. To pass external tests of research output we must write to a high standard while juggling other professional tasks. This may mean changing writing behaviours.

Writing for Academic Journals draws on current research and theory to provide new knowledge on writing across the disciplines. Drawing on her extensive experience of running writing workshops and working closely with academics on developing writing, Rowena Murray offers a host of practical and tested strategies for good academic writing.

This jargon free, user-friendly, practical and motivational book is essential for the desk of every academic, postgraduate student and researcher for whom publication is an indicator of the quality of their work and ability.

Contents

240pp   0 335 21392 8 (Paperback)   0 335 21393 6 (Hardback)

BECOMING AN AUTHOR
ADVICE FOR ACADEMICS AND OTHER PROFESSIONALS
David Canter and Gavin Fairbairn

Becoming an Author is an accessible and engaging toolkit for those working in academia. The authors' wide portfolio of published work in many mediums, has helped them fill the book with their real-life experiences of encountering and overcoming problems associated with becoming an author.

It takes the reader through the process of planning to write through to actually getting down to writing. It covers aspects such as:

- Making your ideas a reality
- Improving structure and style
- Where and how to publish your work
- Managing moral, ethical and legal constraints
- Dealing with publishers

It demystifies all aspects of the move from being an effective student or active professional, to being published. The psychological and emotional barriers are examined as well as clarification of the best processes to get beyond them. The veil of confusion that surrounds the practicalities of publishing in academic journals, or entering the book market place, are outlined clearly.

Becoming an Author is for students, academics and other professionals who want to build their careers, their confidence and their personal satisfaction through publication.

Contents
Preface – About the authors – Publishing without perishing – The author's journey – Varieties of publication – Beyond the blank page – The importance of style – The importance of structure – Using illustration – Moral authorship: responsibilities and rights – Writing for journals – The journal process – Newspapers and other forms of publication – Doing a book – From idea to reality: a book's journey to print – Changing media – Postscript: becoming an academic author – Bibliography and references – Index.

224pp   0 335 20275 6 (Paperback)   0 335 20276 4 (Hardback)